Understanding Your Toddler

Understanding Your Toddler

A Month-By-Month Development & Activity Guide For Playing With Your Toddler From One To Three Years

AYELET MARINOVICH

STRENGTH IN WORDS LLC
MOUNTAIN VIEW, CALIFORNIA

ISBN: 978-1-7321329-2-4

eISBN: 978-1-7321329-3-1

Contents

Introduction

We work hard as parents and caregivers of young children. We work hard to build big brains and great kids, to provide emotional and financial stability for our families, and to create and maintain healthy habits to pass along. With all that hard work, it can be difficult to feel satisfied with the quality and quantity of time we're able to actually devote to simply *being* with our children. Many of us struggle with maintaining balance, finding time, and conserving energy, so we want to maximize the time we have with our tiny humans. We want to find more joy in the journey through these early years of parenthood.

That desire can become somewhat complicated when we're raising people who are, themselves, grappling with big feelings in tiny bodies. Toddlerhood is often marked by the need for independence, a short attention span, difficulty with transitions, and a desire to explore... everything. Finding quality, age-appropriate resources to guide a toddler's learning can seem daunting, and feeling satisfied with the amount of time you're able to be truly present with your child (or multiple young children!) can be a constant challenge.

We *all* want to "succeed" at parenting, but many of us question whether we're doing all we "should" be doing to support our toddlers when their needs and interests seem to be constantly changing, when their newfound ability to move independently means that they won't be able to sit still for more than a few minutes, and when we have to balance playtime with getting "life" done!

We want to shape their behavior so that they become fantastic human beings. We want to keep calm without joining their chaos. And we want to be reassured that we're doing "enough," and doing it "right."

Regardless of who you are, where you come from, what language or languages you speak, you and I (and anyone who considers themselves a parent or caregiver) are each ultimately responsible for raising humans. When we understand more about how humans all over the world develop and learn, we feel more empowered to do the big job of parenting tiny humans.

This book does not aim to cover specific parenting philosophies. This is about our toddlers, and about you. As I did with you and your infant in my first book, *Understanding Your Baby,* I want to provide gentle support to help you understand and connect with your toddler, so you can move *together* through the years of toddlerhood. We mix the developmental research (the science) with the creative ways to support the developmental stages through which your toddler moves (the art).

In so doing, we are going to get to the heart of what it is to be a caregiver of toddlers.

Both infants *and* toddlers learn through observation, imitation, and interaction. When we learn more about what learning and play looks like using very simple materials and strategies, we feel some peace of mind that we all crave as parents. Peace of mind, after all, is what we all want: we want to know that we are doing all we can to raise incredible human beings.

To do that, we look at the four major areas of development: cognitive, communicative, motor, and social/emotional development. Though in my first book, *Understanding Your Baby*, I did not explicitly outline the 4-pillar framework I use to connect with and support a young child within each of those developmental domains, my goal is to do so here in this book.

Journeying Through Toddlerhood

As I write this book, I'm parenting a 5-year old and a 2-year old. Like all parents, I myself struggle with self-regulation, at times I find myself modeling behavior I do not want to see in my children, and I get distracted by the stuff of life when giving them my full attention would be so much more effective. But, like all parents, I'm also human. I've learned to give myself a little grace. I'm learning to forgive myself. I'm learning to put the perfectionist to bed sometimes, and to admit and talk about the fact that I'm not always right, and I don't always make good choices. I do that because I want to teach my children that all of that is part of being human.

I'll never forget the first time I realized my baby was becoming a toddler. He was holding a cracker and playing a game, pretending to give me a bite. When I had the audacity to be playful and take an actual bite... that's when I knew the transition to toddlerhood was upon us. It was the first time he was offended by my actions, the first time he expressed that he wanted to be in control and was not, the first time I did something that made him frustrated. Though part of me wanted to laugh by the utter ridiculousness of crying about a cracker, another part of me thought what a profound moment this was. Here was a person who, up to this point, allowed me to help him engage with the world in the way I saw fit. And in this moment, he was telling me something very clear: if we were going to get through this, he was going to need to have a say.

By that, I don't mean that I was going to have to lay down and simply let him take the reins. I mean that I was going to have to continue to be intentional about the structure I laid out for him, and give him the ability to make choices and control elements within that structure. Things were changing (as they do), and to make room for his growing brain and body, I was going to have to adapt, too.

Here's where that framework I mentioned above helps. If we can find simple ways to support all areas of our toddler's development, we can feel confident that we're doing that big job, and doing it well. So, what are those four pillars to consider? I refer to them as: **Play**, **Talk**, **Sing**, and **Move**. I'll outline what I mean by each of these in detail in the next section, but first let me tell you more about me, and how I came to write this book.

My Professional Background

I want to start by saying that I certainly don't know everything there is to know about toddler development. That said, over the last several years, I've sharpened and deepened my professional knowledge as a practicing pediatric speech-language pathologist. I've mothered my way through two very different early parenting experiences. I've also interviewed countless professionals about the ways we can support both infants and toddlers in the areas of cognition, communication, motor and sensory, and social/emotional development, and I've read a good deal of the developmental research and literature that informs how (and what) we practice as professionals in the world of early child development.

Much of my professional background is in early intervention. I have dedicated my career to working with "early communicators," primarily with infants and toddlers and their adult counterparts. In the world of education, the term "early learning" often refers to children who are not yet school-aged, but who are in the preschool years... but we know that babies are learning from day one (and even before). We know that their parents and caregivers are learning, too.

Those first few years set the stage for the rest of our child's life. Now, I don't say that to add to the incredible pressure we have as parents and caregivers to "do enough" for our children. That weight is already more than sufficiently heavy! In my mind, it's about simplification. We desperately need to simplify our lives. We need access to quality over quantity. Our children need high quality interactions and opportunities to engage with the world, not "the latest learning toy." We, their care-givers, need access to high quality information and high quality inter-actions, and an opportunity to reflect upon what's working and what's not working – not a million mommy blogs and fancy craft ideas on Pin-terest.

When we (as parents and caregivers) feel confident that we have access to resources that actually make a difference, we feel empowered to do the job of raising tiny humans. As an early interventionist, I strive to work within family-centered practice. This means that I help families maximize the opportunities for play and development within naturally occurring, everyday activities, and using materials that already exist within the home. Instead of being the therapist who walks into a fam-ily's home with a "magical" bag of therapy materials, I see my job as that of a facilitator or coach, helping families see the power of routines-based intervention, and focusing on "routines" that are most important to that family. A routine is any activity that is regularly occurring, that has a fairly predictable set of steps, and that has a clear beginning and end. We all engage in different kinds of routines in our homes – caregiving routines (e.g., eating, dressing, washing), play routines (e.g., dance parties, nature walks, book-reading), social routines (e.g., performing a finger play, playing peek-a-boo, tickling), and daily tasks (e.g., getting the mail, putting on shoes before we go outside). When we can identify these and maximize their value, we can make a huge difference within simple activities (that we're already doing)!

At Learn With Less®, we create resources to improve the quality of your family's interactions by sharing easily digestible information that increases your knowledge about early development, and simple ideas to make use of that information. Come join our community of families and help us spread the word about Learn With Less®.

Want to go deeper with me? You can connect on a regular basis with this curriculum and topics related to your biggest challenges in the Learn With Less® Curriculum Online Program: https://learnwith-less.com/online

Want in-person connection? Check to see if one of our licensed Learn With Less® facilitators is hosting classes or workshops in your area! You can find a list of current providers here: https://learnwithless.com/classes

Thanks for making me part of your journey through parenthood,

Ayelet Marinovich, M.A., CCC-SLP

https://learnwithless.com

© 2019 Strength In Words LLC

How To Use This Book

There's no such thing as a step-by-step parenting guide. No two families – and no two children – are the same. This book is not a "how-to" guide to get you through toddlerhood. There's no way (at least, for me) to write a book like that, because I don't much care for "one-sized-fits-all" approaches to parenting. There are, however, universal truths about how humans develop. I've broken these down into 50 little pearls of wisdom, anchored in developmental research and helping you to utilize what you already have: your body, your voice, and a few simple objects (already) in your environment that can be used to help you maximize your interactions with your toddler, and support your toddler's development.

The content of this book can be considered a toddler guide and "curriculum" for parents and caregivers of toddlers from 12 – 36 months (1 to 3 years), delivered in a manner that can be easily consumed by busy, exhausted, often overwhelmed parents. You may be balancing home and work life, you may be raising multiple children, you may be sleep-deprived... you may be all of the above. In this book, you'll find 50 easily digestible "modules" on which you can focus – two for each month of the toddler years. You can download the handy "Understanding Your Toddler: Month-By-Month Calendar" that comes with your purchase of this book (find that and all the other bonus materials here: https://learn-withless.com/toddler-bonus), print it out, and stick it up on your refrigerator or on a wall of your nursery so you'll get in the habit of referring back to this book when you need a gentle guide.

Each month includes two modules for learning about your child's development and what you can do to support it. Each of these modules includes concise "nuggets" of developmental information, paired with ways to integrate ideas from four simple, practical pillars that require little to no materials – one for each of the frameworks I'll outline in the next section. Each module addresses a major area of development, including: cognitive, communicative, motor, or social/emotional development. You can think of this as a semi-monthly "check-in," not simply a list of developmental milestones! This curriculum is based on developmental research and universal guidelines for early learning, and is useful for all families – those whose toddlers are moving along a typical progression of development, and those experiencing (or at risk for) developmental delays.

IN CASE YOU'VE SKIPPED DOWN TO THESE "HOW TO" STEPS, HERE'S WHAT YOU NEED TO KNOW:

1. Head over to https://learnwithless.com/toddler-bonus and download your free bonus materials, including your month-by-month calendar. I don't know about you, but placing a reminder right in front of me is the only way I'll be more likely to use tools and resources in which I've invested. And I want you to use this book!
2. You can jump into the book at any stage. If your child is still in her first year and you're "getting ahead," start from chapter one, month 12. If your child is already 18 months old, go ahead and skip to chapter two (and so on)!
3. Throughout the book, I may refer you to additional resources on the Learn With Less website. The aforementioned link will also help guide you to those resources, where they're listed and broken down by chapter.

That's it! I'll be here for you every step of the way – don't hesitate to reach out on social media! I always love to hear from readers. If you've been inspired by something you've learned or tried, go ahead and use the hashtag #learnwithless – join other families and let us know what *your* family life looks like!

Instagram: @learnwithless

Facebook: @learnwithless

On Early Development And Play

PLAY-BASED LEARNING

We've all heard about "that toddler" who can sit at a table with flash-cards and identify numbers, letters, shapes, colors, and animals. We also hear that we're supposed to talk, play, read, and sing to our young children, that we should be following our child's lead, and that this is how they learn... for many parents hoping to support their toddler's development, it can be tricky finding the balance between unstruc-tured play and what many of us think of as "structured learning" or helping our toddlers reach the more adult-defined "academic learning" milestones.

I had a recent conversation with the mother of a 14-month old, who shared that her biggest struggle when it comes to supporting her tod-dler's learning is finding that balance. She described a mom-friend with a son her child's same age, who could sit and attend to flashcards, who could look at those images and rattle off the names of things... she knew in her heart that *her* son, who would (more often than not) prefer to climb and run and jump, was fully capable of learning... but still, next to his flashcard-toting peer, he "seemed" behind. This story is not unique. Our children have preferences. Our toddlers are extremely busy, curious beings, who excel and flourish in different areas, whose interests vary greatly (often from one moment to the next), and whose abilities in all developmental areas vary widely. The notion that "struc-tured learning" (at a tabletop with flashcards, worksheets, or even books) is *necessary* for toddlers to learn the precursors to academic skills to which we as adults often assign so much value... is a myth.

There are a few things to say here: firstly, toddlers learned to identify objects and label pictures in their environment long before the age of flashcards. And when they learn through experience of the world – with that object or idea, with their body, in real life and in real time... that learning is much more efficient than with a two dimensional picture without context. They learn about the properties of those objects: textures, weight, what it takes in their bodies to control the movement *of* them in space (**motor and sensory**). They connect concepts with objects themselves (**cognition**). Through interaction with another person, they learn the vocabulary (and how to *use* language) within a social context, in social interactions (**communication and social/emotional development**).

Secondly, when we hear a young toddler repeating, labeling, or identifying numbers or colors, we often assign a different kind of internal value to that type of vocabulary, associating it with academic learning or language. But... to a toddler, it's just repeating and imitating another word. If you hold up a flashcard of the number two and hold up a flashcard of a table, you're teaching the same skill: memorization.

It's the *experience* of words, objects, people, and ideas in a variety contexts, settings, and environments that supports your child's learning. It's the *way* they are able to play, the *words* that are used around them, the *musicality* of those experiences, and the *movement* of their bodies that supports what becomes a precursor for academic learning. As adults, we often have a difficult time connecting these things.

You Already Have All The Materials You Need to Play, Talk, Sing and Move

We are already engaging in the kinds of activities that can make a huge impact on our toddler's development (caregiving routines, short play routines, and other daily routines). We also already have the materials we need. Play has been defined as an activity that is done for its own sake, that is process-oriented, that requires and allows for flexibility (on both the part of the child and caregiver!), and that has a positive effect on those involved.[1] Our toddlers learn through this process – through

1. Smith, P. K., and Pellegrini, A. (2008). Learning Through Play. In: Encyclopedia on Early Childhood Development (online). 1-6.

interaction with us and with the objects in their environment. If we can encourage the following, we are doing "what we need to do" to guide our little ones, to stimulate the senses, and to support all areas of learning. Consider adding *more* of the following into each of your interactions with your child:

The Four Pillars Of The Learn With Less® Curriculum:

PLAY:

- Encourage open-ended play and experimentation, ensuring safety with a variety of materials;
- Explore and experiment in a variety of environments using ALL of the senses;
- Forget an end-goal;
- Stay flexible!

TALK:

- Foster an environment that encourages discussion and observation;
- Offer experiences that allow for repetition (and remember that repetition with variation is the gold standard);
- Communicate for a variety of purposes and using a variety of means and modalities (verbal and non-verbal);
- Wonder aloud and imitate your child (her movements, her interests, her vocalizations);
- Offer one step above her ability or one way to rephrase that which she already said;
- Model the behavior you want to see.

SING:

- Add a silly element to an existing experience, add joy into routines, distract or engage with music;
- Energize or calm the sensory system;
- Sing about what you see;
- Find rhythms everywhere and in everything;
- Make music with what you have (your body, your voice, your laun-

dry basket drum)...

MOVE:

- Remember that movement is learning and the very essence of life (even tiny, reflexive movements!);
- Consider various planes of movement (forward, backward, side to side, up and down, diagonal);
- Understand that exploration cannot be contained – and "containers" (large and small) for your child only provide so much – so get outside, change the environment, and change the materials around you.

The Benefits of Open-Ended Play

We all have open-ended play materials lying around our homes and neighborhoods, often in plain view. Open-ended materials (sometimes referred to as "loose parts" are simply items that can be used in lots of different ways and in different environments (say, indoors or outdoors), and can be combined and often redesigned or repurposed by a young child in any way that child or his playmates decide.

These materials often allow children to explore and be inventive in the way they are used... toddlers are naturally inventive, and you might have already noticed that your child is often more interested in the regular objects you have lying around the house rather than the fancy toy that the grandparents purchased for the holidays...

Often, young children end up exploring their environment, taking regular objects, and converting them into toys – a prime example of this is the toddler who explores the kitchen cabinets, taking out his favorite "drum set," a pot and a pan! An older toddler who is engaged in what's called "symbolic" play, or the kind of play that uses objects to symbolize and imitate what they've seen others doing, might take out the same pot, pan, and a wooden spoon, and start to stir, imitating his parents in the kitchen.

Any open-ended material often encourages creative thinking, in that a child must explore its properties and how it might be used.[2] In addition, when you have a house or play area full of open-ended materials, they can often be used together in new and inventive ways. A scarf or a blanket might serve as a great hiding place for a building block. A cork might balance beautifully on top of a wooden block or a toothbrush holder, or fit inside a paper towel roll. A coaster might balance beautifully against another one, and behave as a tunnel for a ball to roll through.

Open-ended materials often encourage problem-solving.[3] What fits where? How can I get this to work that way? Can I get that out if I pull this? Using open-ended materials also tends to save us a lot of money. Not only do we often save money by using common household objects or natural materials instead of expensive electronic gadgets that purport themselves to "teach such and such" skill, our children are going to learn best through exploring, interacting, and imitating us!

Open ended toys are really just materials that your little one can explore, without a set agenda. And when we encourage our tiny people to become more creative, that will serve them well down the road: we encourage them to be active participants in their lives.

What We Need To Understand About Play With Toddlers: It Might Look Different

Adults often think of play in adult notions. We might think of "playing a game," which has rules, follows an often linear trajectory, and depends on others doing things "correctly" to be played. Toddlers play, too, but

2. Torelli, L. (1992). The developmentally designed group care setting: A supportive environment for infants, toddlers, and caregivers. In E. Fenichel (Ed.), Zero to Three child care classics: 7 articles on infant/toddler development (pp. 37-40). Arlington, VA: Zero to Three/National Center For Clinical Infant Programs.
3. Daly, L. & Beloglovsky, M. (2015). Loose parts: inspiring play in young children. St. Paul, MN: Redleaf Press.

they have their own agenda. Playing with them often requires a shift in our own mentality, because they don't have the attention span or interest to follow "rules." For a toddler, play is not terribly linear! When a toddler sees a stack of blocks, she might prefer to knock it down and throw each one, rather than building a tower. When a toddler sees a bookshelf, he doesn't necessarily intend to carefully remove one single book, open it, and read it from cover to cover (with or without you) – though he might, at times! Does that mean they "can't" or "shouldn't" play with those materials in their own way? Absolutely not! In fact, there are layers of skills that emerge over time, through various experiences with those play materials, that build the foundation for skills such as constructing and reading.

What comes first is observation, exploration, imitation, and interaction. This is why you'll often hear educators who work with infants and toddlers (and well into the preschool years) suggest that you "follow your child's lead." If your toddler is removing all the books from the shelf... chances are, she's learning about them. If she's taking all the toys out of the box, she may be comparing and contrasting their properties: how heavy each item is, how much force her body requires to pick it up and move it to the other side of her body, what sound it makes, what texture it has. Young children are constantly experimenting with the world around them – it's how they play, and it's how they learn.

We can model the way we play with an object, giving our toddler the chance to observe and imitate. When he's ready (and when and if he's interested!), assuming his body is able to, he will imitate our actions. We can narrate what we're doing, what our child is doing, provide musical experiences, early literacy experiences, and movement and sensory experiences for our babies. In so doing, we provide our children with the tools to learn, and with an environment that encourages social/emotional development, cognitive development, communication development, and motor development.

Holistic Learning

Infants and toddlers learn "holistically," meaning that although there are various areas of learning and development, they are all very much connected in the first three years of life.

Throughout this period, a child may focus on a certain type of skill or interest in one domain, but process and practice all kinds of information simultaneously.[4] For a further discussion of this topic, please listen to the Learn With Less podcast episode, "**Holistic Learning.**"

The bond that can form simply from being with your young child allows you as the caregiver to start to watch and read your little one's interests, preferences, and behaviors even from the first few months. We tend to start paying attention to (and sometimes obsess over) things like motor abilities and language development during toddlerhood because it becomes very clear who is hitting what milestone first… it starts to become very obvious when a child is able to crawl, walk, run, and jump, or when she's using gestures, words, or full sentences.

We have to remember that these capabilities don't just magically appear the day we witness them in our children – they're the result of layers of learning, practicing, and problem-solving. That ramp that your toddler obsesses over at the park is where she learns about balance, force, velocity, proprioception (perceptual motor development), what changes if she puts her arms up when she moves downward (cognitive development), whether she'll be understood if she points, looks at, vocalizes, and/or says the word, "up" when being pushed in the stroller past the ramp (communicative development), and whether you're paying attention when she looks up and smiles at you at the bottom each time (social/emotional development).

The point is, we have to learn to give our young children opportunities to experiment and learn, and we need to give our toddlers the benefit of the doubt that they are learning all the time.

4. California Department of Education, California Infant/Toddler Curriculum Framework, Sacramento, 2012, pg. 133.

Questions and Concerns About Development

The information and activities we will discuss in this book are largely applicable to both typically developing toddlers, as well as those with developmental delays and special needs. The ideas presented here are for informational purposes only and are not medical advice. This curriculum is not meant to replace an individualized treatment plan developed as the result of in-person assessment, clinical observation, and collaboration between therapist and caregiver.

If you are concerned about your child's development or functional abilities, please seek information from your child's medical provider, or seek out the services of a developmental pediatrician or local pediatric therapist within a specialty area (e.g., physical therapist, speech-language pathologist, occupational therapist, etc).

Although I am a registered and licensed speech-language pathologist, this curriculum is not a place for therapeutic recommendations or interventions to address specific delays or diagnoses. The ideas presented here are intended to be used for play in a supervised setting. If you have questions or concerns about presenting any activity to your toddler, speak with your child's medical professional beforehand.

Always ensure that you are present and attentive when presenting an activity to your toddler. Strength In Words LLC is not liable for any injury incurred while replicating an activity found within this book.

Finally, if you are concerned about whether your child is engaging with the world in a developmentally appropriate manner, consider whether your child can *hear* the world around him. In order to participate fully, your child must be able to use all his senses to connect with the world. If your child cannot hear, he can't imitate your verbalizations, he likely will not be interacting with you verbally to the same degree as his same-aged peers, and he can't observe and listen to your words.

1. 12 - 17 Months

Within this chapter, I'll suggest additional resources for you to explore on the Learn With Less website. You can find all of those resources organized by chapter here: https://learnwithless.com/toddler-bonus

12 Months old: Form and Function

Form and Function (Cognitive Development)

Your little one enjoys exploring objects in different ways to understand their properties. She might pick up an object, shake or bang it, or carry it with her. Most likely, she is starting (or will start soon) to associate familiar objects with their function – e.g., a spoon is something you put in your mouth when eating, a brush is something you put in your hair. She learned that these objects are used in this manner by watching others perform these tasks, and interact with objects.

Research suggests that toddlers of this age imitate not only what they see adults do, but also consider the adult's intention of that action when replicating the behavior themselves. In a 2002 study, researchers studied what 14-month olds did when they watched an adult turn on a light with his forehead when his hands were occupied. When asked to turn off the light, the 14-month olds in the study overwhelmingly used their hands to turn the light off, even though they had observed the adult using his head.[1] The implication is that children within this age range (12-15 months) take the intention into consideration when they imitate an adult, not just the behavior.

WHAT YOU CAN DO:

1. G. Gergely, H. Bekkering, and I. Király, "Rational Imitation in Preverbal Infants: Babies May Opt for a Simpler Way to Turn on a Light After Watching an Adult Do It," Nature 415 (February 2002): 755–56.

When your baby shakes or bangs on an object (for instance), she is experimenting with the object and the way it is used, considering concepts such as weight, texture, etc. Give words for the objects, for their properties, and for her actions!

PLAY

- Offer a few household items to your baby in a play context

  - You might consider objects found in the kitchen, living room, bedroom, bathroom, etc), and see what she does with them.

- Pick them up and inspect them yourself

  - Model traditional use of them
  - Experiment with them in different ways (e.g., stacking them, placing them inside larger objects, sorting them).

- She will likely be engrossed in her own play, and may or may not imitate you in the moment.

  - Follow and accept what she does!

TALK

- Give words:

  - For the objects (e.g., "it's a ball," "I have a coaster!")
  - For their properties (e.g., sticky, heavy, blue, big)
  - For her actions ("you're throwing it!," "you put it in! You put it in again!")

SING

- Choose a familiar simple tune and sing the melody using a single word to replace the lyrics
  - ◦ The name for the object she's holding
  - ◦ The action in which she's engaging
  - ◦ The fact all the objects are going "in" or "out," etc.

MOVE

- Explore your surroundings by taking a walking/crawling tour of the room you're in and the objects around you.
- When you use an object (whether in play or in "real life"), give your baby a turn with that object, or with a safe version of that object (or other objects that do something similar or that are found in the same area).

12 Months Old: More Than Labels

More Than Labels (Communicative Development)

As young toddlers start to use more communication (both verbal and nonverbal), it's easy for us as adults to become "drill sergeants" when our intention is to help our young children learn. We often naturally ask our little ones to label objects or people (in pictures or in the environment) – sometimes to elicit their communication, and sometimes to solicit their attention. This can easily turn into a "labelling habit," where we're stuck in a rut, asking the same question – "what's this? What's that?"

Getting creative by asking different kinds of questions, creating playful experiences (rather than just pointing and naming), linking objects and people to previous experiences, are all great ways to provide a "language-rich" interaction. In this way, you shift the focus of the activity from a labeling activity into a true communicative activity between the two of you – so you're both part of the activity, instead of you directing the activity. This is also more likely to capture your child's attention for a longer period of time, as it is a more natural engagement and interaction, vs. "testing" your child (inherent in the "drill sergeant" way of demanding they answer us). When we use language functionally, we help our children communicate – not only do we model appropriate use of language, we model how to start conversations, and take turns during conversations!

WHAT YOU CAN DO:

Point out objects that you notice, and take turns as you would in any conversation!

PLAY

- Using a picture book, a magazine, or other images in your environment, examine what you see:
    - A picture on a bus stop
    - A picture on a cereal box
    - Pictures on t-shirts in the laundry pile
- Talk about what you notice, and about what your child is noticing.
- Do something silly with the object or image (e.g., tickle the person in the picture, give it a hug, ask it if it's hungry), then turn to your child, pause, and observe his reaction.

TALK

- Talk about:

    - What your child is doing
    - What you're doing
    - What you see and notice
    - What your child notices

- Ask questions of all kinds – don't be afraid if they're rhetorical questions, and after you've paused to allow for some kind of answer (whether or not it comes!), you can answer what you think!

    - Who is in the picture?
    - Where are they going?
    - How will they get there?

- Alternatively, ask your child a question, giving him a choice of two answers (e.g., do you think the dog is hungry or thirsty?) – provide a gesture for each so your child can imitate your gesture and/or your words.
- Accept your child's level of communication, and model one step above!

SING

- Make up a song about:

    - The pictures you see
    - The actions you're performing
    - The way others are feeling

- Insert these words into a familiar melody.

MOVE

- Act out the gestures, movements, or actions of the people or objects in the picture.
- Move to another room or to another environment (e.g., outside from inside) just like the objects/people in the picture, when appropriate.
- Go on a hunt to find a similar object in your home, giving your child contextual experience with that item.

13 Months Old: Environmental Freedom

Environmental Freedom (Motor Development)

There is a wide range of typical motor development milestones – both gross motor (e.g., walking) and fine motor (e.g., using utensils). A child's preference for movement exploration is also individual. Some children have a strong need to move their bodies and some are more content to observe and stay more sedentary. These differences appear to be governed by both internal preferences (e.g., personality traits) and external preferences (e.g., physical experiences in which they want to engage).[2] By respecting these individualized differences, we honor our child's inclinations and build off their natural strengths.

When our young children are able to choose what and how to play with objects around them, they are more likely to explore their environment.[3] In a safe environment with interesting options, they are able

2. California Department of Education, California Infant/Toddler Curriculum Framework, Sacramento, 2012, pg. 12
3. Bergen, D., Reid, R., and Torelli, L. (2009). Educating and Caring for Very Young Children: The Infant/Toddler Curriculum (2nd ed.). New York, NY: Teachers College Press.

to reach, move, and explore! This allows them to experience the world from both a movement and sensory perspective, integrating information and discerning ways certain experiences are similar or dissimilar to other experiences they've had.

WHAT YOU CAN DO:

Provide your baby with safe play spaces on the floor to explore and investigate her environment so she can roll, crawl, walk, and stretch, and limit the use of equipment that restricts your baby's movement!

PLAY

- Create play temptations and "tableaus" (e.g., set up or arrange a few materials to entice exploration) in your child's natural environment.
- Set up objects in novel ways (e.g., place swim goggles or a hat on a teddy bear), tempting your child to explore new things in her environment independently.

TALK

- Talk about what your child is doing, and how she is moving her body.
- Narrate her actions, and/or yours!
- Wonder aloud about what each of you might do to get to an object on the other side of the room, or how you might get into an object that requires dexterity.

SING

- Use the melody of a short song to sing about your actions (or the actions of a stuffed animal).
- Bang on a drum ("real" or repurposed, such as a laundry basket or an empty box).

MOVE

- Encourage your child to reach from one side of her body to the other (by modeling, or setting items up on both sides of your child's body).
- Take turns hiding behind furniture and create a social routine around a peek-a-boo game.

13 Months Old: Self-Identity

Self-Identity (Social/Emotional Development)

Your child is clearly communicating his mood, his feelings and his desires – through verbal and non-verbal means. He is building his awareness of self by independently choosing and exploring materials. This sense of self is emerging, and will continue to emerge as he starts to link concepts and build his use of language around his own individuality within the context of social relationships.[4]

---

4. Rochat, F. (2003). Five Levels of Self-Awareness as they Unfold Early In Life.Consciousness and Cognition 12 (2003) 717–731.

When you follow his lead, and give words for the actions he performs, the way he plays, and the people involved, you encourage his sense of self within the context of a social relationship. Being present with him (as in, being near him and encouraging his exploration, without directing him) as he explores the world helps to lay the foundation for him to build expectations about others' behavior and about his own ability to explore his interests.

WHAT YOU CAN DO:

Watch or engage with the materials he's using, and provide the words for the objects, actions either of you are performing, or the relationship between the objects. Observe what he does, and model ways to play with the same materials, without expecting that he do the same.

PLAY

- Explore a few safe items together, finding ways to play games like peekaboo, relate the objects to your body or to your child's, and investigate their properties:

  - Kitchen items (e.g., pots, pans, mixing bowls)
  - Bathroom items (e.g., towels, an empty paper roll, a mirror)
  - Natural objects (e.g., leaves, sticks, pine cones)

TALK

- Integrate words about various body parts (as your child learns the vocabulary for his body parts, he is able to both understand and express the difference between his body and yours).
- Pair a gesture (pointing, signing, nodding, clapping, etc.)

and spoken word for what you're expressing
- When you consistently model that multiple modes of communication can be used, you provide your child with a variety of ways he can imitate you!

SING

- Let the rhythm take you!
- If your child is banging on mixing bowls or using a stick to make sound along a grate, turn on the music or sing a song and imitate the beat.

MOVE

- Move in and out of view of a mirror, playing a game of peek-a-boo, or experimenting with only showing an arm or a leg

    ◦ Make it extra fun by moving your extremity in a silly way or pretending it talks to your child in the mirror.

- Take notice of footprints or handprints left (in water, paint, or mud) – help your child integrate the knowledge that they are not only an entity in the world, but also that they leave traces on the world!

14 Months Old: Musical Patterning

Musical Patterning (Cognitive Development)

Music is a very natural opportunity to hear and engage in patterns. Many pieces of music are based on a sequence that often repeats (in the melody and/or lyrics). When a child is able to anticipate a pattern and "sequence" a series of events, she is also inherently building math and literacy skills!

When we link a sequence of events to a specific routine activity (e.g., getting ready for a meal requires a series of steps: washing hands, rolling up sleeves, sitting down at the table), we create connections for our child to help her learn to anticipate what will happen next. In addition, we create an expected set of circumstances that helps her deal with transitions. Adding an element of musicality that we perform each time helps to solidify this even further, as it provides an additional recognizable pattern.

WHAT YOU CAN DO:

Sing songs or read books that are repetitive and that have rhyming words, or reference visuals in the environment, to help your child learn to anticipate what comes next.

PLAY

- Adding "visual supports" to your environment in the form of pictures can provide a clear indicator for your child about what will come next.
- Print out photos of a process from start to finish (or use pictures from a magazine that represent a thought or process).
    - Place these in areas with which you associate a particular routine (e.g., a picture of a shoe on the wall next to the closet where you keep your shoes)
    - This allows you to easily reference the next step in a familiar routine to help your child become success-

ful.

TALK

- Honor your child's attempt to communicate, and the idea that in any particular moment, she may not be interested in answering a question you ask.
- Remember to pause and wait for her to process what she sees (e.g., a picture in a book), what she hears (a song, or the fact that you've paused expectantly), and what she needs to do with her body next.

    ◦ *"The window on the bus goes... [pause] up and down! – I saw you move your arm up – yes! Up and down..."*

SING

- When singing a familiar song, make use of expectant pause by pausing before you finish a familiar line in a story or song, as above.
- Remember to give your child plenty of time for her to process.

    ◦ You may need to wait 10-20 seconds for a reaction before you ask a question again or let her know how you're "reading" her silence
    ◦ This sounds like a very long time in the life of a tod-dler who may appear to have either moved on or

completely zoned out. Try to remember that your child's brain is processing information in a different way from yours!

- *"I'll ask again because I didn't see you answer! It's late and we're tired. Twinkle, twinkle, little... yes – you pointed to the star!"*

MOVE

- Add a gesture for each step of a process, modeling that which you want to see your child imitate.

    - For instance, if you're preparing to wash hands, you might rub your hands together saying (or singing to the tune of *Here We Go Round The Mulberry Bush*):
    - *"Now it's time to wash our hands, wash our hands, wash our hands / Now it's time to wash our hands so we can eat our food!"*

14 Months Old: Gestures and Words

Gestures and Words (Communicative Development)

Typically, a child of this age is starting to use some "real" words. Keep in mind, a "real" word does not need to be produced "correctly" to be considered a word. As defined in my first book, *Understanding Your Baby*, a true word meets the following guidelines:[5]

- **Consistency**: you hear it over and over again, often in the same context
- **Use in appropriate context**: you hear it in the same context across different situations, often using non-verbal cues (e.g., your baby says "nana" while pointing to and looking at the banana
- **Recognizable speech sounds**: the word may not be pronounced correctly, but the "essence" is there – e.g., your baby says "Wawa" for "water"
- **Spontaneous utterance**: your baby utters the word spontaneously, as in, on his own and not in imitation

Whether or not your child is expressing himself through words, we can encourage early word development by focusing on the words we use in routines in which we engage day in, and day out. Use a few words in context, short sentences, and utilize repetition.

We often see nouns develop first, because they name the familiar people, places, and objects (things) all over the child's environment, to which they receive regular exposure. Young toddlers often develop strong preferences for certain people, places, and items. We can be intentional about using these words within a context that is repeatable (such as a caregiving routine, a short daily routine like putting on shoes before going outside, or within a play routine like a finger play or tickling game).

Within this age range, it's common for frustration to increases because a child's understanding of language (receptive language) often outweighs his ability to use language (expressive language). Young toddlers are often very motivated to communicate specific thoughts, but may not yet be able to coordinate the fine motor movements necessary to say the words they'd like to use.[6] We can help fill in the

5. McLaughlin, S. (2006). Introduction to Language Development (2nd ed.) Clifton, NY: Thomson Delmar Learning.
6. Goodwyn, S. W., & Acredolo, L. P. (1993). Symbolic gesture versus word: Is there a

gap for our children by becoming more intentional about the ways in which we use both gestures and words. We can model various types of gestures, and pair them with a spoken word. This provides a multi-modal approach to communication, and to use of symbolic language, providing an auditory experience (hearing the word), a visual experi-ence (seeing the representation of the word or thought), and a tactile and movement experience they can imitate, should they desire. When your child can experience understanding of a word in various ways, he knows he can use any of those modes of communication to get his own point across to you.

WHAT YOU CAN DO:

Be mindful of your child's preferences! Within short moments of play and regular caregiving routines, model use of those words in context, both verbally and non-verbally, when possible.

PLAY

- When your child expresses an interest in an object (whether food, a clothing item, a household object, or a "traditional" toy), take time to use the name for that object in context!

    - Label it
    - Talk about what your child is doing with it
    - How is it moving or where is it going
    - Who is using it

modality advantage for onset of symbol use? [Electronic version] Child Devel-opment, 688-701. From Academic Search Premier.

TALK

- Make observations about what's happening, and use various types of gestures

    - Referential gestures (where you're referring to an object by pointing to it, moving your body towards it, and/or looking at it)
    - Representational gestures (using a sign for the word, or moving your hand as if you're rolling a ball when you say the word "roll")

SING

- Take a familiar tune and adjust the lyrics to sing about the object and what's happening with it!
- Singing a song like "*Mary Had A Little Lamb*" is a great "plug and play" song that you can use to adapt to your child's name and the object with which he's playing!

MOVE

- Model to your child the use of various gestures, pairing the gesture with the word.
- Gesturing requires fine motor movements and control, but can also include full body movements such as walking or crawling to the other side of the room toward a desired person or object!

15 Months Old: Fine Motor Play

Fine Motor Play (Motor Development)

Your child is learning so much more about what her body is capable of, and is fine-tuning many skills – especially those that include "fine motor" skills, or movements with small muscles that often involve more precision. Your child practices her fine motor skills each time she manipulates objects with her hands, but also with her other extremities, such as her legs or head.

When you find opportunities during caregiving routines and within everyday play to help your child use her fingers and hands to manipulate objects of all kinds, you're playing into your child's interests and preferences, and you're more likely to be building attention skills, as well.

WHAT YOU CAN DO:

Offer activities that require use of your child's smaller muscles, encouraging her to manipulate objects and participate in routine events.

PLAY

- Using tools or fingers themselves, offer materials for art making (e.g., paper, paint, tape, stickers, water on cement) or building materials (e.g., sticks, blocks, rocks, bricks of diaper wipe containers).
- Encourage opportunities during caregiving routines:

    ◦ Eating/drinking (e.g., hold utensils, serve oneself, or hold a cup)
    ◦ Bathing (squeezing a washcloth, transferring water to a cup or bowl)
    ◦ Dressing (offering or lifting a leg and pushing it through her trousers)

TALK

- Provide words for what your child is doing, but don't be afraid of participating in the play, in parallel (next to her, but not necessarily "with" her).

  - Talk about what you're doing
  - Wonder aloud about what might happen next if you experiment with the object in a certain way
  - Problem-solve aloud how you might fix something
  - Talk about how you're imitating the movements she's making

SING

- Making a musical experience doesn't necessarily mean singing an entire song!

  - When you (or your child) build a tower or place a few objects in a line, you might say a word such as "more" or "up" each time you add another
  - Move your intonation up a note each time you add another

MOVE

- Hide smaller items under other objects for your child to find and discover.
- Set up a few items of various properties (texture, shape,

weight, etc) for your child to experiment with and move as she sees fit!

15 Months Old: Empathy and Social Sharing

Empathy and Social Sharing (Social/Emotional Development)

Researchers find a big difference between babies who are 15 months and babies who are 18 months with regard to understanding "other" minds. In one particular study, 18-month olds gave a researcher what she wanted (not what they wanted), whereas 15-month olds simply gave her what they liked and preferred.[7]

This tells us that "typically developing" 18-month olds are beginning to understand that not everybody likes the same thing, and also that they can help people get what they want! We start to see some very smart negotiation tactics – essentially, "how do I make you happy while also making me happy?"

Toddlers are notoriously "challenged" when it comes to sharing, because they are learning about the concepts of possession, desire, and pleasure. They are also learning that they can enact the change in the world to get the things they need! We do not tend to see children younger than 3 years old that truly (consistently) understand the concept of sharing and turn-taking within a social context with a desired object. However, we do see 18-month olds starting to learn specific aspects of these skills.

7. Gopnik, Alison. (2010). How Babies Think. Scientific American. 303. 76-81. 10.1038/scientificamerican0710-76

WHAT YOU CAN DO:

We cannot legitimately expect our young toddlers to share on their own, but we can help them start to connect the dots by giving them opportunities to practice.

PLAY

- Practice taking turns in play:

    - Throw the ball back and forth
    - Play instruments (you drum, then he drums)
    - Explore vocal play back and forth (singing or making silly noises)
    - Ask questions, and then pause for an answer
    - Stack blocks (you, then him)

TALK

- Provide the language for sharing: *my turn, your turn, first you; then me, give, take, mine, yours, ours, etc.*
- Talk about the feelings involved to help your toddler form perspective-taking abilities

    - *"Look how sad she is – now she doesn't have a toy to play with! Can we find another for her?"*

- Praise "negotiation" tactics

    - *"You gave him another toy – that made him feel good!"*

SING

- Pause during a familiar song or book, and give your child a chance to fill in the missing word or gesture.

    - If he does, that's great!
    - If not, continue on and try again in the next verse or on another day
    - In this way, you're providing the structure for turn-taking, and teaching your child, modeling interactional behavior

MOVE

- Follow your toddler (physically) in his exploration of the environment and of objects.

    - If you're in a park or on the sidewalk, imitate his movements or grab another item just like his.
    - Offer it to him, asking him if he wants a turn.

16 Months Old: Imitation and Attention

Imitation and Attention (Cognitive Development)

Infants and toddlers often imitate in order to learn more about the people and the world around them, or to solve a problem. When trying a new skill, we know that young children are more likely to imitate acts they see us doing when those tasks are of moderate difficulty –

research suggests that they analyze the level of difficulty before they even attempt to imitate us.[8]

This relates to what is known in the field of psychology (put forth by psychologist Lev Vygotsky) as the "zone of proximal development," or the distance between what a child already knows and what is completely unknown. Within this "zone" are activities that interest young children, and which can be done with guidance and encouragement. When given the appropriate level of assistance, the adult can slowly offer less and less assistance until the child can perform the task independently.[9]

As referenced in a previous module, recent research also suggests that young toddlers also imitate based on what they think adults intend to do. In other words, they are already starting to infer what we are trying to do and why we are trying to do it – for instance, we push a button in order to turn on a light.[10]

WHAT YOU CAN DO:

When you are performing household tasks, caregiving routines, or sitting in focused play with your baby, narrate the actions you're performing, and tell her about your intentions.

PLAY

- Assuming she is physically able, your child will imitate you

8. Harnick, F.S. (1978). The Relationship between Ability Level and Task Difficulty in Producing Imitation in Infants. Child Development, 49(1), 209–212. http://doi.org/10.2307/1128610
9. Vygotsky, L. S. (1978). Mind in Society: the Development of Higher Psychological Processes. Cambridge, MA: Harvard University Press.
10. G. Gergely, H. Bekkering, and I. Király, "Rational Imitation in Preverbal Infants: Babies May Opt for a Simpler Way to Turn on a Light After Watching an Adult Do It,"Nature415 (February 2002): 755–56.

when she is ready and interested (and when you've created a "moderately difficult" level of interest for her)

- Until then, try to model new ways of doing thing in a play context without expecting her to do them the same way, and without doing them for her!

- Think about ways to simplify or reproduce parts of tasks to encourage her participation.

TALK

- If you see or hear your child imitate something you said or did, try doing it again, varying the actions or steps slightly.

  - This may help to keep your baby interested in what you're doing, and provide another related task from which to imitate and learn!

SING

- Add environmental sounds to what you're doing, exaggerating your voice, its natural intonation or vocal contours (moving up and down or down and up), and the sounds themselves.

  - For example, while you're making the bed, *"Shaaaake! Shaaaake! Shaaaake the sheet! Whooooooooosh! The sheet goes over the bed! Now we'll finish making the bed."*

MOVE

- If your baby appears intrigued with what you're doing or the way you're playing (e.g., watches your movements as you build a tower with blocks, open a sheet over the bed, or pour water from a cup into a bowl), offer her a turn.

  ◦ Consider how to make the task slightly easier or slightly more difficult.

16 Months Old: Growth In Vocabulary

Growth in Vocabulary (Communicative Development)

A toddler's understanding and use of vocabulary (as well as sentence structures!) will grow when he is exposed to those words in context. That means that when he observes an adult using specific words in meaningful situations (over a period of time), he starts to learn that vocabulary. When observation is paired with interaction – whether the child is directly and actively engaging with or listening to another person during play, caregiving routines, or other routines of life – our children can engage directly with the vocabulary within context, learning by watching and using other senses (touching, listening, moving, etc).

As we already discussed, young children are more likely to imitate acts they see us doing when those tasks are of moderate difficulty – so when we give them multiple experiences with a word AND multiple ways to express that word (by saying the word, signing or gesturing toward the representation of the word, using pictures in the environment or in books), we make it more likely that they will start to imitate us in whatever way they can!

WHAT YOU CAN DO:

Offer a wide variety of new (and familiar) vocabulary to expand on your child's experiences, and increase the likelihood that your child will retain verbal information around those experiences.

PLAY

- Focus on a theme based on your child's interests.
- If you notice your child enjoys the song *"Twinkle, Twinkle, Little Star,"*

  ∘ Start pointing out stars in the environment
  ∘ Find photographs of stars and place them around the room
  ∘ Find or make a book with stars on the pages and point them out

TALK

- When your child points to something:

  ∘ Imitate his gesture
  ∘ Add the word
  ∘ Then add a little bit more information, providing context around the word, and building upon his interests with additional information
  ∘ For instance, if your child points to a baby in a picture book, you can point and say, *"Yes, it's a baby! You see the baby! Here is the baby's nose! Where is your nose?"*

SING

- When you sing a familiar song:
    - Act out the actions
    - Adapt the words so you're singing about the activities at hand (in your own environment)
    - Choose a word to sing "on" (using a familiar melody, simply replace all the words with *that* word)

MOVE

- Explore your surroundings and narrate what you're doing, or what you're child is doing, as you go along.
    - Don't feel like narrating the whole experience? That's fine!
    - Just point out what's of interest to your child as he explores – *"You found a flower! Mmm, I wonder how it smells? Sniff! Mmm! So nice! Want to try? No? Oh you're touching it – those are the petals – so smooth!"*

17 Months Old: Big Movement, Big Brains

Big Movement, Big Brains (Motor Development)

You may have noticed your toddler repeating a task over and over (and over) again. The old adage, "practice makes perfect" applies to toddlers, as well. The thing is, it isn't always outwardly obvious what exactly your child is practicing.

You may be walking along, trying to give your child a few minutes of movement by allowing her to walk alongside you (even though you wish you could go more quickly), and suddenly notice that your child has stopped, or is attempting to turn around. "What on earth?" you might think... And though you'd prefer to continue on your journey, the very slight incline on the road has caught your toddler's attention, and she's keen to explore it.

Though this may not be the time or place (and if it's not, you be the judge of that!), but your child is likely integrating old and new experiences, potentially even connecting concepts and words, to the movements she's making. She may be perceiving new things about how she needs to hold her body to balance when managing a slight variation in the ground. She may be exploring the concepts of "up" and "down." She may be figuring out something else, entirely! Research suggests that the development of both perceptual motor and other motor behaviors (as in, movements and the ways our bodies perceive those movements through our senses), occur within the context of our experiences, often in the context of social relationships.[11]

WHAT YOU CAN DO:

Ensure your child has plenty of opportunities for movement and movement experimentation (play) in a variety of environments.

PLAY

- Whenever possible, provide opportunities for exploration. Leave a few minutes earlier than you planned, so you have time to explore a new (or familiar) place.
- Provide time outdoors and indoors, whether dedicated "playtime" like going to the playground, or grabbing a few

11. Diamond, A. (2007). Interrelated and Interdependent. Developmental Science 10, no. 1: 152-58.

extra minutes for meandering through the park or along the sidewalk on the way to the grocery store.

TALK

- Narrate what's happening – if your child appears to be practicing something repetitively, provide words for what she's doing.
  - If she's going up and down a slight gradient, simply say *"up!"* when her body goes up, and *"down!"* when her body goes down.

SING

- Add a familiar tune, or imitate the rhythm of her movements.
  - Add a train noise as she moves along, and stop singing/chanting when her body stops
  - If she notices you are making music along to her movements, she may find this entertaining!

MOVE

- Follow the leader!

- Try what she tries, whether she's exploring something large or small
- Comment on the experience

17 Months Old: Emotional Language

Emotional Language (Social/Emotional Development)

Research suggests that young toddlers around the age of 18 months pay attention to emotions directed at them, as well as emotional information directed at others, and that they use both kinds of information to make decisions and inform their behavior.[12]

Not one of us is the "perfect" parent. As parents and caregivers, each and every one of us has "lost our cool" (sometimes, more often than we'd like to admit). The good news is that each time either of us has a strong emotional reaction, we have a chance to make use of this moment as a learning moment. Within each of these opportunities, your child is not only learning about his relationship with you, he's also learning about how people express and regulate their emotions, how and in what ways others around him control their impulses, and how to behave in a social context.

WHAT YOU CAN DO:

The way you speak to your child, to others, and to yourself, guides his behavior. Calling attention to the feelings of others (in front of you, in pictures or in books) gives your child an emotional vocabulary!

12. Repacholi, B. M., & Meltzoff, A. N. (2007). Emotional eavesdropping: infants selectively respond to indirect emotional signals. Child development, 78(2), 503-21.

PLAY

- Acknowledge negative experiences of even inanimate objects within a play context.

  ○ If a stuffed animal (or even a toy vehicle) falls or hurts itself, provide the language
  ○ *"Ouch! That hurt – poor train, it fell off its tracks, how sad."*

TALK

- When you witness "big feelings" in others (around you, in pictures, or in books), talk about them!
- Make comments and predictions about what might be going on:

  ○ *"That baby is crying. She might not want to get into her stroller. Maybe she's not ready to go yet. That sometimes happens to you!"*

- Acknowledge (when possible) when you have big emotions.

  ○ When you do this, you model your own process of self-regulation.
  ○ When you experience big emotions in front of your child, take a moment and regroup: start small.
  ○ Simply state what's happening around you. *"I'm feeling frustrated and tired. I had just folded all that laundry, and now it's fallen on the floor."*

***Great Resource:* Learn With Less podcast episodes:**

- **"Labelling Emotions"**
- **"How Infants and Toddlers Learn About Emotions,"** featuring an interview with Dr. Laura Markham

SING

- Incorporate facial expressions into your musical repertoire.

  - Look at pictures
  - Look in front of a mirror
  - Look at each other
  - Sing about feelings

On my album, "Strength In Words: Music For Families," I've adapted the finger play, "*Where Is Thumpkin?*" to "*Where Is A __ Face?*"

- Search in a magazine or book for a "sad" face
- Find (or make) a "sad" face, and wonder aloud why that person might be feeling that way.

MOVE

- Model the way movement can help either of you shake off a feeling (literally).
- Once you've acknowledged the "big" emotion, suggest a dance party, a literal "shake-off" of that feeling, or "chase" your happy place around!

2. 18 - 23 Months

Within this chapter, I'll suggest additional resources for you to explore on the Learn With Less website. You can find all of those resources organized by chapter here: https://learnwithless.com/toddler-bonus

18 Months Old: Experiments With Cause & Effect

Experiments With Cause and Effect (Cognitive Development)

Toddlers of this age are often very interested in exploring how things work, and enjoy the problem-solving that results in understanding cause and effect. Utilizing materials that support this exploration of cause and effect is a wonderful way to support cognitive development.

Remember that open-ended materials – actual "toys" or repurposed household items – often allow young children to explore and be inventive, figuring out how they work and move, creating new ways to use objects, and using them together. For instance, a clump of play-doh might balance beautifully on top of a wooden car, or fit inside a shape sorter. A puzzle piece might fit inside one cup, but not another. Toys that light up or that make noise when a button is pressed are also teaching cause and effect; however, that is essentially all they teach: there is only one way to use them, so they don't tend to encourage the kind of thinking fostered by open-ended materials that can engage your child in an exploration of cause and effect (and much, much more).

WHAT YOU CAN DO:

Offer a variety of materials for play. Include materials that yield an interesting result when acted upon, and that encourage "if, then" questions ("if I do this, then what will happen?").

PLAY

- Offer materials from your home that twist or move in interesting ways, fit inside each other, or are differently shaped (e.g., lids on snack containers, measuring cups, mixing bowls).
- A collection of objects you might find in a hardware store (e.g., latches, light switches, tape, knobs, PVC or other pipe parts that fit together) can be explored when offered in a bowl, or attached together on a "latch board" (a piece of wood onto which a variety of latches, fasteners, and simple gadgets are affixed).

TALK

- Wonder aloud:
  - What is happening
  - What you or your child might do next
- Model silly things like placing objects on your head or hiding them under your armpit.
- Work in natural opportunities for building vocabulary
  - When you place an object on a body part and say it aloud, you're focusing on body parts!
- Provide opportunities for your child to tell you (either verbally or using gesture) where she'd like an object to go.

SING

- Musical instruments can be made from almost anything.
- Exploring the various sounds that objects make in isolation or together can be done by shaking, tapping, blowing, etc.

MOVE

- Bring one object at a time from one side of the room to the other (and back again, if so desired)!
- Explore, compare, and contrast objects from the outdoors and indoors (and how they look or feel in each environment).
- Go on a "hunt" for soft things (for instance), allowing you to point out various textures along the way.

18 Months Old: Social Language

Social Language (Communicative Development)

Your child is likely starting to understand and use language more and more. Although there is so much focus on a child's vocabulary at this age, the way your child uses language socially is also a large part of her ability to communicate.

When we communicate for a variety of different reasons using a variety of means (non-verbal and verbal), we model appropriate communication for our children. Talking through events can help your child when an activity is less familiar or less preferred, and models to our child that internal commentary can also be external – overtly allowing our children to experience different elements of a conversation.

WHAT YOU CAN DO:

Model how to start a conversation, take turns during an interaction, and ask and answer questions – simply by engaging in all those parts of conversation with your child, yourself!

PLAY

- Create opportunities within play for starting a conversation – include greetings in your play with dolls, with other inanimate objects that might "talk" to each other (e.g., two vehicles), or in song.
- Take turns during an interaction, and model the asking of questions, pausing (waiting for someone to answer), and the answering of questions.

  ◦ This might look something like, *"Well, hello there, green car! Where are you going?* [pause] *Oh, you're heading to the library? Let's go together!"*

TALK

- Talk about what you're doing during daily routines.

  ◦ Narrate what you're doing or what your child is doing, telling a story about what's happening in your lives.
  ◦ Narrate the process of what's happening: *"I need to wash my hands now. Turn on the water – wash, wash, wash, scrub! Turn it off and dry – pat, pat,*

pat."

SING

- Turn narration of your day into a song.

    ◦ Sing about the process of a familiar routine, or simply add an element of rhythm to your process: *"pat, a pat, a pat-a-pat-pat. Shall we do it to you, too?"*
    ◦ Adding a simple shift in the rhythm of your voice may help your child engage.

MOVE

- When possible, give your child the opportunity to "do it herself."
- Build independence into familiar routines to:

    ◦ Give her an experience with an activity while she hears the words
    ◦ Build on her own self-concept and sense of confidence
    ◦ Allow her to apply the language of the day to her own actions

        ▪ This also allows your use of pronouns to change, "first I did it, now you do it!"

19 Months Old: Keeping Up With Tiny Humans

Keeping Up With Tiny Humans (Motor Development)

As your toddler becomes more mobile, he will explore his environment more and more. This may affect what he's interested in exploring and doing, and he may not want to stay in place for long. You may find that your once specific "play area" is now all over the home.

Your home *is* his territory! This is where he feels most comfortable engaging in daily activities of life – which is a form of play. Because he wants to explore and play all over your home, play can quickly shift into less "productive" (by our adult standards) activities, such as unrolling toilet paper or pulling down curtains. Creating areas for play (sometimes referred to as "yes spaces"), offering your child an alternative "version" of a less safe option, or closing off areas of the home that are "off limits" may be part of your child-proofing experience.

WHAT YOU CAN DO:

Your toddler wants to move on his own terms, and has his own ideas in mind. Redirection is key, here, both physically (in terms of where play and exploration can occur) and in terms of meeting the underlying desire or need your child has.

PLAY

- If your child is determined that the toilet paper in the bathroom should be made available to him, offer a full roll to him in a play setting (and depending on your child's level of determination close the door / place a child lock on the bathroom when it is unavailable).

  - Alternatively, replace the desire to unroll the paper with an emptied tissue box, a wipes container, or a shoe box, full of something acceptable to pull out (such as scarves or napkins).

- If his desire is to pull on something hanging from the wall or ceiling:

  - Make an attempt to replace that activity with another form of "heavy work" (providing heavy input to the joints and muscles, by pulling, pushing, etc)
  - Transition into a peekaboo activity in another place

- Meeting your child's physical or emotional need within a specific activity will create a higher success rate for you when attempting to distract or redirect!

TALK

- Provide a narrative for what your child is doing.

  - Comment, ask questions, observe... but don't feel the need to bombard your toddler with language, either!
  - Remember to provide an opportunity for more silent listening and observation. Embrace the pause after you ask a question.

- There is no hard-and-fast rule for "how much" or "how little" to make conversation.

  - If you find you're a more naturally quiet person, try adding a few opportunities to narrate.

- If you find your child is unresponsive to your many questions, or you feel like you're bombarding him, try adding more silences!

SING

- Adding musical elements to your play can help in redirection or distraction, and can signal both the start and end of a routine (and transition to a new one).
- Try adding a greeting song to your repertoire in moments you haven't previously used one.

    - For instance, if your child seems to be wandering around the home, make the exploration more purposeful by greeting each (available!) room and everything in it within reach, as you arrive, and then, again, as you leave.

MOVE

- Exploration *can* be redirected.
- Try moving more quickly or more slowly, or moving heavier or lighter things.
- Make available spaces more interesting by:

    - Rotating out toys (making some available or more obvious)
    - Creating pillow or blanket "forts"
    - Making other special spaces and obstacle courses

Great Resource: Learn With Less blog post, "DIY Special Space Parachute"

19 Months Old: Cooperation

Cooperation (Social/Emotional Development)

Research suggests that elements of cooperation (such as working together to solve a problem, imitating actions, etc.) between toddlers and their peers start to emerge at the end of the second year of life. Some research has found a dramatic increase in cooperative activity between the ages of 20 – 24 months of age.[1]

We often have unreasonable expectations of our toddlers when it comes to subjects like sharing and cooperation. It can be frustrating to find that on some occasions and in some situations, our children seem to have an understanding of what it means to be cooperative and a desire to share and play together with others (whether peers or adults), and at other times, they seem to "forget" or become incapable of sharing and cooperation. They even appear to be intentionally obstinate.

We must remember that skills like these are complex, require a deep understanding of social rules, and a strong ability to regulate emotions... which are all very much emerging skills in our toddlers.[2] They need opportunities to practice, and positive modeling, if we want them to attain mastery – if we want them to be successful!

WHAT YOU CAN DO:

Model and call attention to cooperative acts when playing with your child and when engaging in everyday activities in your home and in the community.

1. Eckerman, C., Davis, C., & Didow, S. (1989). Toddlers' Emerging Ways of Achieving Social Coordinations with a Peer. Child Development, 60(2), 440-453. doi:10.2307/1130988
2. Brownell CA, Ramani GB, Zerwas S (2006) Becoming a social partner with peers: cooperation and social understanding in one- and two-year-olds. Child Development 77: 803–821.

PLAY

- Imitate your child!

    ◦ Do what she does, and do it together.
    ◦ Do the same thing she does, and add another element (by changing direction, adding another word, etc).

- Model sharing, and hand things to your child.
- Find opportunities for turn-taking in play (e.g., with building toys, in pretend play, or rolling a ball back and forth).

TALK

- Acknowledge aloud when your child is cooperative or gives you a turn / shares with you or others – let her know how this makes you feel!
- When your child cannot be socially cooperative, offer an alternative (for her or for yourself), and state aloud how this might solve the problem at hand.

SING

- Sing songs *about* sharing

    ◦ Give stuffed animals / dolls / other play objects their own "turn" to sing or be sung about

        ▪ For instance, create a verse in *"Old MacDonald*

Had A Farm" about each of them

MOVE

- Encourage pretend play and social routines in which you each take turns engaging with each other

  - Feeding
  - Drawing
  - Scrubbing
  - Using small or large movements

20 Months Old: Pretend Play, Social Play

Pretend Play, Social Play (Cognitive Development)

You may have noticed that your child's play is evolving as he grows. The ways our children can move and communicate are changing, and the ways in which they engage with play materials also changes. We can support their growing brains through play.

Pretend play is a form of play in which a child transforms objects into "pretend" objects that symbolize experiences in which they have engaged. For instance, your child might pick up a block and "pretend" it is a toothbrush, piece of soap, or hairbrush, reenacting parts of familiar caregiving routines. He might "pretend" to feed a stuffed animal at the table, just as he feeds himself (and watches you feed yourself)!

Engaging in pretend play supports complex symbolic thinking (one object "symbolizes" another, or symbolizes the reenactment of a sequence of steps).[3] It can also support and enhance emotional intelligence, self-regulation, and the ability to communicate with others, as it requires those involved to communicate with each other using communicative skills (words, gestures, and objects) to tell a kind of story.[4][5][6]

WHAT YOU CAN DO:

Ensure there are plenty of open-ended play materials that can support pretend play.

PLAY

- Remain flexible in your own thinking about what objects "are"or "could be,"and pay attention to the way your child is using objects symbolically.

  ◦ The lid of a box might become a comb
  ◦ A block may be used as a cup
  ◦ A book may become a tunnel

- Follow your child's lead when playing with objects, and model new ways to use and put objects together!

3. California Department of Education, California Infant/Toddler Curriculum Framework, Sacramento, 2012, pg. 110.
4. Berk, L., & Winsler, A. (1995). Schaffolding Children's Learning: Vygotsky and Early Childhood Education. Washington DC: NAEYC.
5. Ziegler E, Singer D, Bishop-Josef S. Child's Play: The Roots of Reading. Washington, DC: Zero to Three Press; 2005.
6. Kagan, S. & Lowenstein, A. (2004). School readiness and children's play: Contemporary oxymoron or compatible option? In E. Zigler, D. G. Singer, & S. Bishop-Josef (Eds.), Children 's play: The rools ofreading (pp. 59-76). Washington. DC: Zero to Three Press.

TALK

- Recall and reenact previous experiences and familiar experiences within play.
- Use two toy cars / stuffed animals / dolls (or whatever it is your child loves to play with!) and reenact the series of steps you follow when engaging in a familiar experience that happens regularly, such as changing a diaper or bathing.
- Talk through the steps, sequencing them aloud. Wonder aloud what you might need to use next, ask your child if he wants to take a turn helping.

SING

- Sing through the steps of a process.
- Make a whole set of instruments from objects in your home and play a song together or accompany your child's favorite album.

MOVE

- Create special spaces for and with your child using pil-lows, sheets, boxes.
  - Move in and out of them
    - Playing peek-a-boo
    - Bringing things in and taking them out

- Creating a reading nook within which you can simply lounge

20 Months Old: Book-Reading Routines

Book Reading Routines (Communicative Development)

Researchers have found that a child's engagement and interest in book reading can be highly dependent on the context of adult support. When children of this age become familiar with certain routine behaviors *within* the act of book reading, they are more likely to engage. Some of the behaviors that might encourage a child's response include a parent or caregiver's attempt to initiate interactions through motivation (e.g., "look at this!"), pointing at a picture, asking questions, labelling pictures, making comments (e.g., this car is red, like ours), and providing feedback to a child's communication (e.g., "that's right, it's a car!"). Toddlers of this age often initiate interactions and respond to the adult by using gestures (e.g., pointing, waving), labelling, and commenting.[7]

This research confirms what we already know: that following and "playing to" a child's interests, remaining flexible, and creating more playful and conversational experiences out of book reading is often more likely to engage, stimulate, and keep a child's focus and attention than simply reading the words on the page.

WHAT YOU CAN DO:

7. Adriana G. Bus, Jay Belsky, Marinus H. van Ijzendoom, Keith Crnic, Attachment and bookreading patterns: A study of mothers, fathers, and their toddlers, Early Childhood Research Quarterly, Volume 12, Issue 1, 1997, Pages 81-98, ISSN 0885-2006, https://doi.org/10.1016/S0885-2006(97)90044-2.

Engage directly with the text and the pictures when reading with your child, relating them to your child's real life experiences, and follow your child's lead when it comes to engaging with books, without expectation.

PLAY

- Forget the traditional end-goal of "getting through" a book from cover to cover.

  - Instead, explore the pictures, take a picture walk, make inferences about the pictures, and make the experience different every time!

- Take turns on the page

  - At times, model labelling and commenting
  - At other times, wait for your child to show you what she's interested in

Great Resource: Check out the Learn With Less podcast episode, **Wordless Picture Books**

TALK

- Try different strategies such as:

  - Exploring and finding similarities between the pictures
  - Relating pictures to real-life experiences
  - Commenting on emotions or other aspects of the pictures
  - Labelling and making environmental (including animal) sounds

SING

- Sing a song about one of the characters, or adapt a song you know about a similar theme

  - Does the book feature a bus? Try singing a verse of *"The Wheels on the Bus"* to your child to solidify the connection between the word and the song...
  - If the next page is about a car, sing about the wheels (or some other aspect) of the car!

MOVE

- Is your child more interested in removing the books from the shelf?

  - Try stacking them together into a pile
  - Find "all" the covers with animals (or all the blue colors, etc.)
  - Sort the books by size (big ones and little ones)
  - Count the books

21 Months Old: Tower Building

Tower Building (Motor Development)

If you look at a milestone checklist outlining skills that are developmentally appropriate for an 18-24 month old, chances are, you'll see "builds a tower of blocks" listed. Building and stacking objects reflects a young child's ability to mentally form a goal and attempt to meet it by repeating an action sequentially.

This requires several skills, including perceptual information (under-standing, for instance, how to grasp and hold the shape, size and weight of the blocks, and where to place them on top of each other to achieve a sense of balance), and the correct sequence and power of movements to complete the actions.[8]

WHAT YOU CAN DO:

Encourage the act of building, stacking, removing, and placing objects "in" other objects, and offer a variety of materials with which you can do this.

PLAY

- Start building a tower of blocks, rocks, pieces of wood, dia-per wipe containers, or snack storage containers, and offer a "temptation" for your child to get involved.
- Alternatively, offer a few small objects that differ in prop-erties (such as shape, size, texture, and weight) that can be placed inside a bin, basket or bowl (or a variety of con-tainers)!

TALK

- Talk or ask questions about the various aspects of your building materials or your variously sized/shaped objects

  ○ *Where can we put this?*

8. Chen, Y. P., Keen, R., Rosander, K., & von Hofsten, C. (2010). Movement planning reflects skill level and age changes in toddlers. Child development, 81(6), 1846-58.

    ◦ *This one is small, and that one is big!*

- Encourage building and pretending with the objects.

SING

- Each time one of you stacks another block on top of the next, say or sing a word or phrase (e.g., "up," "more blocks") in a slightly higher pitched tone each time.

MOVE

- Go on a hunt around the home for objects that fit inside your basket or bowl, and then line them up along the floor together, or stack them on top of each other.

21 Months Old: Imitation

Imitation (Social/Emotional Development)

From day one, infants appear to engage in imitative acts.[9] As a child

---

9. Jones S. S. (2009). The development of imitation in infancy. Philosophical transactions of the Royal Society of London. Series B, Biological sciences, 364(1528), 2325-35.

grows, we see more and more imitative acts emerge as she acquires more motor, cognitive, social, and communicative skills.

Not only do we, as humans, imitate others, we also learn to recognize when we are being imitated by others. We often innately imitate each other to connect ourselves with another person (often adopting another person's postural, vocal, and gestural habits). Around the age of 18 months, toddlers are building the foundation of this understanding that others are at times "like them," and start to use inferencing based on others' actions. In other words, they use the behavior of others to make judgments about the other person's mental and emotional experience. This is the basis for empathy, and developmental researchers believe that imitation and empathy are intrinsically linked.[10]

WHAT YOU CAN DO:

Engage in imitative acts! This also gives you an opportunity to let go of the expectation that your toddler should imitate you – instead, imitate your child or those around you!

PLAY

- Use a mirror to imitate each other.
- When reading a book, imitate the actions or facial expressions of characters in the story.

10. Meltzoff, A. N., & Decety, J. (2003). What imitation tells us about social cognition: a rapprochement between developmental psychology and cognitive neuroscience. Philosophical transactions of the Royal Society of London. Series B, Biological sciences, 358(1431), 491-500.

TALK

- When your child says something, affirm and/or acknowledge what he said, and then say it in a different way.

    ◦ For instance, if your child says something like, *"Mama up!"* to request that you hold him
    ◦ You might say, *"You said, 'mama up!' You want me to hold you! Mama, hold me! Hold me please, Mama!"*

SING

- When singing songs:

    ◦ Replace an action in a song with the word for what your child is doing
    ◦ Substitute a word in a song with the word for what your child is pointing *to* (e.g., if your child is pointing at the chair, sing the word, "chair!")

- You can do this with any melody!

MOVE

- Take turns imitating each other's movements

    ◦ If your child is simply walking around the room, walk around behind him!

22 Months Old: Categories

Categories (Cognitive Development)

As toddlers start to understand that everything "has a name," they also make more connections between things they see, people they meet, and experiences they have. In other words, your child's exploration of an object by how it feels (in her mouth, in her hands, between her toes), the sounds it makes, the way it moves, and its visible features are all integrated into her understanding of how the world works.

In the early stages, young children understand categories much more broadly (e.g., there are animals, and they are different from people, which are different from furniture). A child who has started using vocabulary might refer to all animals as "dog" at first. These kinds of over-extensions are typical of early language output.

WHAT YOU CAN DO:

Offer items or pictures in play that are grouped together by a certain common feature (e.g., color, texture, shape, size) or by type (e.g., animal, vehicle, body parts, etc).

PLAY

- Fill a shoebox, mixing bowl, or short basket with a few items that fit into the category of your choosing for your child to explore.
- Some ideas to get you going include:
  - Things that are wooden (e.g., a mixing spoon, puzzle piece, block)
  - Things that are green (e.g., a coaster, book, scarf)
  - Natural objects (e.g., a leaf, pinecone, piece of bark)
- Create an image library using magazines, illustrations

from books (line drawings, vintage drawings, photographs, etc), printed images from the internet.

- ○ Find images of everyday objects, that are inspirational, or that you find interesting to look at

Great **Resource: Learn With Less podcast episode, "3 Ways To
Use Routines In Play,"** an interview with speech-language
pathologist Lia Kurtin of Speech & Language At Home

TALK

- · Narrate, narrate, narrate.
- · Give your child the words for what she sees and touches.
- · Point out:

  - ○ What she's doing
  - ○ What she's holding
  - ○ How she is moving something
  - ○ What the texture is like

- · Another term for this is "parallel talk," as in, you're talking
in parallel about everything you see your child doing in
front of you.

SING

- · Within musical experiences, we can reinforce movements
that represent or refer to actions and other types of
words.

- When we use short songs or rhymes that can be easily repeated, or songs with repetitive phrases, we get to model the word again and again.
- We can model words in various categories (whether they're actions, animals, objects, etc) through gestures and signs.

MOVE

- Place images or objects around the home, make category books with images (place them in sheet protectors inside a small binder or keep them in a box), or act them out.

  - For instance, point to the body parts on each other
  - Narrate what you're both wearing
  - Lie on your back and do bicycle legs like the bicycle rider in a photograph

22 Months Old: Pausing Power

Pausing Power (Communicative Development)

Many of us "pause" in our conversation to mark the idea that it is someone else's turn to speak or offer an answer. Using pausing as a strategy to entice your child to communicate can be very useful. When we pause expectantly before saying part of a phrase, we're using a strategy called a "cloze procedure." You may already be doing this with your child without thinking about it, in daily caregiving routines (like washing, dressing, etc), in musical activities when singing familiar songs, or in reading experiences with nursery rhymes or other books.

Caregiving routines and play-based interactive experiences are not only opportunities for repetition, allowing your child to anticipate what's coming next, but they are also opportunities to introduce the idea of ritual to your child. Even if this is simply something you say each time in a silly voice, a song you sing on your way to the bathtub, or a favorite book or poem, these moments become special bonding and interaction time, in addition to predictable opportunities that offer comfort and security.

WHAT YOU CAN DO:

Take an inventory of the types of rituals you might already be engaging in (you may be largely unaware you're even doing them!) and think about other simple little ways to add little phrases to your daily care routines.

PLAY

- Book reading activities are wonderful opportunities – especially when reading those with repetitive phrases.
- Books with repetitive phrases naturally lend themselves to use of the cloze procedure, if we:

    - Leave out the final word or other familiar words in the repetitive line
    - Pause to wait for either a gesture or sign, or the word, before stating or modeling it, ourselves

Great Resource: **Learn With Less podcast episode, "The Power of the Pause"**

TALK

- Whenever you sit down or set up a meal together, you

might say, *"Ok, what do we need? A bib and a plate!"*
- If you start saying this at every meal time, your little one may surprise you by pointing to the objects he sees in his vicinity before you say the phrase, or may respond when you pause – *"What do we need? A bib and a ____"* by gesturing, vocalizing, or verbalizing.
- Whatever he does, you can say, *"That's right! A plate!"* making sure to provide a verbal model or reinforce the adult pronunciation, and validating his response at whatever level he was able to give it to you.

SING

- Familiar songs are wonderful ways to incorporate a pause and elicit language.
- Your child knows what's coming if his favorite song is, *"Twinkle, twinkle, little... ____."*
- All you have to do is look at him and smile expectantly.

    ○ If he doesn't fill it in, that's ok – smile and give him a chance to do it again in a few minutes or the next time you sing the song together!

GreatResource: **Learn With Less DIY blog post, "Lift-The-Flap For Language Book"**

MOVE

- You might use the same phrase when you get into the car

and put on your child's seat belt

- ◦ For instance, *"Arm in, arm in… click!"*
- ◦ Alternatively, when you're heading down the slide, counting, *"one, two… three!"* Or *"ready, set… go!"*

23 Months Old: Big and Heavy Work

Big and Heavy Work (Motor Development)

You may have seen your child fully engaged in pushing a chair across the floor, pulling a laundry basket down the hallway, or rolling a stroller down the road. There's a reason he is focused, resolute, and fully committed.

There are three main sensory systems in the body that lay the foundation for sensory and motor development: the vestibular system (which controls balance and coordination), the proprioceptive system (which provides input to the joints and muscles, helping us understand more about where our body is in space), and the tactile system (what our skin tells us when we are exploring different sensations).

When our children move and push things that are heavy, big, or awkward, their bodies receive maximal input to the muscles and joints. When we provide our children with the opportunity to move their bodies and move objects in their way (e.g., along the hallway, down a path), we allow them to fully feel what their bodies can do, and we allow them to engage and work their muscles, their coordination and perceptual motor abilities, and their sensory system.

WHAT YOU CAN DO:

Many of the best ways to incorporate activities that involve "heavy work" are to simply embed them into everyday activities. If you start to

watch your child, you may find that she is already finding these oppor-
tunities.

PLAY

- Use materials already available in your daily life, and allow your child to participate at whatever level they are able.
- Remember that the idea is not to aim for perfection of a task; rather, we're looking for ways to involve our children in physical activity, allowing them to participate and engage with you, building their confidence, and building the bond of being together with you.
- Think about opportunities that allow your child push her body to its maximal effort in these ways:

  ◦ Climb
  ◦ Carry
  ◦ Hold
  ◦ Pull
  ◦ Push
  ◦ Suck
  ◦ Blow

Great Resource: **Learn With Less DIY blog post, "Heavy Work Activities Inspired by MamaOT"**

TALK

- Be a cheerleader, and make positive, declarative comments about your child's independence and ability to manage handling these objects.

  ◦ Instead of simply praising, tell him about the quali-

ties you see in him
- ◦ *"You're working really hard! I like that you keep trying even when it's not easy! You can let me know if you need help."*

SING

- Move along with your child as you walk, march, pull, or push along objects, and add a rhythm.
- A marching song (such as *"The Ants Go Marching"*) can create a great transition into the beginning or end of an activity.

MOVE

- If you're in the grocery store, your child can pull or push the grocery cart or basket.
- If you're in the backyard, he can hold a watering can and water the plants, hold or pull a rake, or move a hose from one place to another.
- If you're on the playground, any of the pushing, pulling, or climbing equipment your child can engage in at his own level is great for "heavy work" activities.

23 Months Old: Social Stories

Using Social Stories (Social/Emotional Development)

As humans, we are multi-sensory learners. Some of us learn best when we are aided by lots of visuals, and some prefer more tactile experiences, but we can all understand that there are benefits to providing multiple ways to learn. Adding a visual to support learning, whether it's an object you can touch, a photograph, or a drawing, can help guide all of us through our daily life, whether within routines at home, at daycare / preschool / work, and out in our communities.

Sometimes, visual aids can be helpful for rehearsing what will happen next, especially if they are new or less familiar experiences, or for helping to represent a transition that will soon be coming. This practice, sometimes referred to as creating "social stories," has been used for many years, and is a wonderful tool to help toddlers with "self-regulation," or that ability to manage impulses or emotions. As we know, toddlers are learning that they can enact change on their world through expressing their own opinions.

Social stories provide context within a visual – through photos in the environment, within a book, on a white board – that tell a story about what's happening in their world. When we provide this type of visual storytelling opportunity for our children, we give them a way to see what's coming next, to anticipate a series of steps, and to talk about and interact with their world in a way that gives them control over what, otherwise, might be an abstract concept. This, in turn, helps them regulate their emotions, and provides a way for them to feel more secure and stable in the ever-changing process of the day. You can use these stories and visual aids within routines, within transitions between activities, and with preferred or less preferred activities.

Originally, social stories were created to support social/emotional development of children with autism spectrum disorders,[11] as these children often experience communication challenges within social situations. Toddlers of all developmental levels often experience difficulty with self-regulation, impulse control, verbal language, and social skills.

WHAT YOU CAN DO:

Create a visual representation of objects, experiences, or people in your child's world. Find ways to incorporate actual objects or pictures (photographs, drawings, images from magazines or printed from the internet) into both familiar and less familiar routines and events in your child's life.

PLAY

- A few minutes before you know you'll need to transition into a new activity that necessitates an end to open-ended play with your child:

  - Grab or point to a visual representation of an object (or an object that represents an upcoming transition, such as your shoes)
  - This lets her know both with your words and a physical representation (or "visual") that in a few minutes, you'll be moving to the next activity

TALK

- Walk your child through the visuals you're using, provid-

11. Gray, C. 1994. The new social story book illustrated edition. Arlington, TX: Future Horizons.

ing words so that you're "front loading" your child with what's coming next.

- ∘ Work these into routines – getting ready to go to daycare, getting in the car, getting dressed, or heading to the library

- Be the judge of how many "steps" in the story you want to highlight, and pair a visual with each one.

  - ∘ For instance, grab a piece of paper and a pen, and draw a shoe, a door, and a car (don't worry about your artistic abilities – simply focus on the experience of going through the information together, and of talking through what the objects are)
  - ∘ Talk to your child about how, in the next few minutes, together you'll put on shoes, open the door, and get in the car

Great Resource: **Learn With Less podcast episode, "A Story of Raising & Working With Children With Autism,"** featuring an interview with physical therapist Leslie Hayden

SING

- Often, music can help ease a transition.
- In addition to a visual representation, pairing a particular melody or words in a sing-song voice can cue your child for what's coming next.

MOVE

- When your child knows the sequence of a set of steps to get to the next familiar activity, she can be more involved and more independent (and more cooperative)!

  - For instance, if part of getting out the door is grabbing the keys from the table or hook where they're kept, your child can be the one to walk to or point to the keys to tell you what's next.

3. 24 - 29 Months

Within this chapter, I'll suggest additional resources for you to explore on the Learn With Less website. You can find all of those resources organized by chapter here: https://learnwithless.com/toddler-bonus

24 Months Old: Pre-Operational Stage

Pre-Operational Stage (Cognitive Development)

In the first few years of life, between newborn to about two years old, infants and toddlers explore the world by coming into direct contact with it, primarily through sensory and motor experiences. What this means is that young children learn primarily through movement, touch, and other sensory experiences. What these little ones are doing by touching, listening, looking, moving through space, and tasting or mouthing... is learning. They are constantly processing this world through their experiences. Psychologist Jean Piaget called this stage the "sensorimotor stage" in his model of cognitive development[1] (which, through the years, despite contention over specific details, remains a basic model for our understanding of early development).

What happens at age two? Piaget called the next stage of cognitive development the "pre-operational" stage (which carries through the bulk of early childhood, from age two through age seven). Within this stage, a young child starts to use symbols (such as words, signs, or gestures) to represent people, objects, environments, thoughts, and ideas they experience in the world. Reason and logic are still emerging skills, and our toddlers are still quite ego-centric, meaning that the "self" is all important. Young children are learning how to integrate information about others, and attempting to understand how others think and per-

1. Piaget, J. (1970). Science of education and the psychology of the child. New York: Viking

ceive the world... but this process of learning about others' perspectives, of understanding the notion that the world may look different to different people... that has to do with the ability to think outside of oneself.

This is a big part of why pretend play (such as reenacting situations, interactions, or stories) and other symbolic play (or the use of one object to represent another, like using a wooden block to pretend to brush one's hair), are such important areas to encourage in young children. When a child has the benefit of experiencing the world within his body and brain from an early age, he has a larger collection of experiences to draw upon in terms of the vocabulary and personal experiences. He has integrated all of those experiences into his knowledge of the world.

WHAT YOU CAN DO:

Expose your child to a varied set of rich experiences of the world – through vocabulary, sensations, environments, partners, etc.

PLAY

- When our children repeat actions, explore through touch, and process different kinds of sensory information, they are learning through play.
- Take opportunities to explore new and varied materials (objects that vary in shape, texture, size, color, etc, and those that are natural and human-made).
- Explore new environments, as well as new elements of familiar places:

  - The hallway in your home can become a raceway for cars or for blowing cotton balls
  - A dirt mound in your neighborhood might become a great new place to find earthworms after a rain storm
  - A series of puddles in the back yard or on your walk

home might be a great splash pad in the right clothes, or when you know it's easy to find dry ones

TALK

- Though you don't need to always be an active play participant, providing the words for what you're doing alongside your child or what your child is doing

  - How he's doing it and what he's doing it *with,* for instance, are great ways to connect the concepts he's exploring with the words for them

SING

- Since your child is already processing a variety of sensory experiences at the same time, try to pick out one element (in this case, an auditory experience), and make it more interesting

  - Accentuate the rhythm of part of the activity
  - Highlight an environmental sound

    - The dripping of a faucet – "drip, drip, drop!"
    - The flutter of a butterfly – "flutter, flutter, flutter-by, butterfly!"
    - The sounds of a nearby machine – "vrrrrr, vrrrrr"

MOVE

- Take a "nature walk" wherever you are (simply head out-side in the right clothes):

  - Experience the breeze
  - Move in the rain
  - Touch hard and soft and rough things
  - Pick flowers for a friend
  - Making and observing body shadows

24 Months Old: Practice Into Symbols

Practice Into Symbols (Communicative Development)

The word "play" is often associated with imagination, music, laughter, connection, togetherness, and enjoyment. We can play with toys, play music, and play games. There has been a substantial amount of research done on early play as it relates to infant, toddler, and early child development, and there appears to be a typical sequence to the type of play in which young children engage. Play is closely linked to cognitive as well as communicative development (regardless of which of the various researchers' theories you follow), and can be seen as a way for children to explore, make sense of, and find pleasure in the world.

Generally, from early infancy until about 18 months of age, young children engage in what researcher Jean Piaget described as "practice play." This is essentially a period of time when the child is learning about herself and the object at hand through the means of her senses. The child explores how she can change the environment in some way. This might look like the following: shaking a rattle, blowing bubbles/raspberries, putting objects in the mouth, playing peek-a-boo, taking objects out of a box, screeching happily and watching others' reactions.

Between the ages of 18 months to 2 years of age, a transition starts to emerge, and play starts to become more sophisticated, turning into "symbolic play." This stage of play lasts until roughly 3-4 years of age. Your child starts to make use of the objects around her to represent things she sees in her world, people she has met, interactions she's had or witnessed. She may use an actual object (e.g., a parent's lipstick) or an object that symbolically represents that object ("smearing" a LEGO brick onto her mouth).

This symbolic play stage also overlaps with a deeper entry into an era of symbolic communication. Typically, a child starts to combine two words together by this age, enabling her to express her thoughts, desires, needs, and opinions more eloquently. This often results in what's called "holophrastic" or "telegraphic" speech, wherein your child expresses a full thought by simplifying a whole phrase into an efficient shorter utterance, such as "Mama up" ("Mama, pick me up!") or "No Wash" ("I don't want to wash my hands right now").

WHAT YOU CAN DO:

Support this entry into a more symbolic era by playing with your child and engaging in everyday activities together.

PLAY

- Connect everyday objects with their use, and find ways for your child to participate in everyday routines, performing them with actual objects or representational objects.
- Take turns using a comb or brush in the morning, then reenact that experience with a doll, stuffed animal, or other toy using an actual comb or something that loosely resembles that shape/size (e.g., a long wooden block, a plastic piece of corn, an empty paper roll).

TALK

- Talk about what you're doing together, and communicate within your play for a variety of purposes.
- Ask questions about what's happening, make requests for your child to hand you something, make comments about what you think or what you see, use appropriate greetings in your play, provide the words for what you or your child is doing.
- Acknowledge what she says, and repeat it back to her first the same way, and then in a different way or with one more element.

  - For instance, if she makes a comment like, *"big car,"* you might say, *"that's right! It's a big car! It's a really big car! It's huge!"*

SING

- Create silly songs about what you're doing, how you're moving, or what you'll do next.
- Adapt the words of a song or rhyme, or simply put your words into a rhythm.

  - If you're both standing in the bathroom brushing teeth, you might sing a song that simply uses the word "brush," or that adds in pronouns
  - *"You brush! You brush! You brush, brush, brush your teeth. I brush! I brush! I brush, brush, brush my teeth!"*

MOVE

- Symbolic play includes opportunities for all kinds of movement

  - Structure building (e.g., with blocks, sticks, or pillows)
  - Pushing objects around (e.g., your child's stroller, a doll's stroller, a chair or laundry basket)
  - Water and sand play (e.g., pouring and sifting, transferring, mixing, and creating "concoctions" and "recipes")

25 Months Old: Get Up and Move

Get Up and Move (Motor Development)

A higher level of sedentary behavior (and lower physical activity levels) has been linked to delays in motor development in young children.[2] Researchers have posited that physical activity improves physical health, and that it positively supports both cognitive and social/emotional development.[3]

Many countries around the world have released recommendations regarding physical activity and sedentary behavior, including Canada, Australia, and the United Kingdom. These guidelines generally recom-

2. Cliff DP, Okely AD, Smith LM, McKeen K. Relationships between fundamental movement skills and objectively measured physical activity in preschool children. Pediatr Exerc Sci. 2009;21:436–49
3. Timmons, B. W., Leblanc, A. G., Carson, V., Gorber, S. C., Dillman, C., Janssen, I. et al. (2012). Systematic review of physical activity and health in the early years (aged 0-4 years). Applied Physiology, Nutrition and Metabolism, 37, 773-792.

mend that children between the ages of 1 – 4 years of age should spend no more than 60 minutes at a time seated or restrained (e.g., in a car seat, high chair, or stroller), and should spend at minimum 180 minutes partaking in any level of intensity with regard to physical activity per day.[4][5][6][7]

Each family's relationship with the decision about dealing with screen time is highly individualized, but decisions should take these recommendations into account. We also know that the motor skills required to press a button or manipulate objects on a screen are not the same as moving and manipulation of physical objects. Part of the reason for this is the difference between interacting within a two-dimensional screen vs. a three-dimensional world. When "stacking" blocks on a screen, a toddler does not receive any of the sensory input required to move her body in space, does not determine the weight or size of the objects.

WHAT YOU CAN DO:

Limit sedentary time, and remember that "high tech" is not always better.

PLAY

4. Tremblay MS, Leblanc AG, Carson V, Choquette L, Connor Gorber S, Dillman C, Duggan M, Gordon MJ, Hicks A, Janssen I, et al. Canadian physical activity guidelines for the early years (aged 0-4 years). Appl Physiol Nutr Metab. 2012;37(2):345–69.
5. Tremblay MS, Leblanc AG, Carson V, Choquette L, Connor Gorber S, Dillman C, Duggan M, Gordon MJ, Hicks A, Janssen I, et al. Canadian sedentary behaviour guidelines for the early years (aged 0 –4 years). Appl Physiol Nutr Metab. 2012;37(2):370–91.
6. Move and play every day. National physical activity recommendations for children 0–5 years. Australia Government: Department of Health; 2010.
7. Start active, stay active: a report on physical activity for health from the four home countries' Chief Medical Officers. United Kingdom: Department of Health, Physical Activity, Health Improvement and Protection; 2011.

- Explore the environment, create experiments with existing materials (consider "if we do this, then what will happen" questions), and remember that your child may know what she wants to do with an object...

    ◦ It may not be the "right" way to play with or use that object, but you can trust that she's learning about it!

- Offer variations and let her lead the way.

TALK

- Make observations about what you're each doing, and why that may be happening.
- Make predictions about what might come next.

SING

- Add actions into your songs

    ◦ Sing about what you're doing or how you're moving
    ◦ Hum a tune at the speed in which you're each moving

MOVE

- Exploration of the environment and of materials *is how*

your child learns.
- Place tempting materials at different levels for her to find (higher, lower, inside something else, under something).
- Encourage movement from side to side, up and down, forward and backward, on the diagonal...

25 Months Old: Social Cognition

Social Cognition (Social/Emotional Development)

Pro-social behavior (essentially, the ability to be social with others) is highly linked to "social cognition," and the ability to take another person's perspective. As your child journeys through the toddler years, it is natural that this is an emerging skill – easier in certain situations than in others!

Emotional intelligence, or the ability to understand oneself and understand others, requires the development of what psychologists call "theory of mind." Essentially, theory of mind is the ability to take another person's perspective, and to understand that not everyone shares the same thoughts, ideas, and feelings as you do. There is a fairly clear progression of abilities that help a child to form his emerging understanding of theory of mind, and, again, it develops over time, over the first five years of life (and beyond)! Imitation, sharing, testing behaviors, empathy, pretend play... these are all involved in the development of theory of mind, and are all skills and abilities that develop layer upon layer.

As adults, we tend to forget that our children's learning doesn't happen overnight. We tend to focus on "the day my child accomplished" something, instead of the many, many steps and experiments and failures and learning moments that formed the ability to successfully accomplish that task.

One of the skills considered part of social cognition is the ability to pay attention to others and to imitate them. This is why building routines, engaging interactively, creating consistency within those interactions, and repetition with variation, are all so integral for your toddler's brain development: it informs him about communication, feelings, movement, patterns and sequences...

Your toddler may be performing experiments to test causality, consistency, and correlation. When he throws a toy, he may look at your face to gauge your response. While your first instinct might be to discipline, consider what kind of scientific experiment he might be performing. Your consistent response is often what your toddler is "testing" when he looks to you for a reaction: "If I throw the toy in this room, will she react differently? How about if I throw it harder? Higher? Into the basket?" Our ability to be as consistent as possible, firm, loving, and patient, is what slowly shapes their behavior into that of a prosocial, upstanding, contributing member of society. Their skills are emerging, and we cannot force the progression.

It's not until later on that children really start to integrate and think about what others might be feeling and thinking (vs. a toddler experimenting with what this might be like or look like). There are other factors at play as well, such as the ability to regulate one's own emotions and actions, which are also emerging simultaneously. Toddlers might be "able to" or interested in sharing every once in a while, but not likely all the time. Empathy might be visible sometimes, but not all the time.

WHAT YOU CAN DO:

Encourage the positive behavior you see in your own child, support the emergence of perspective taking and empathy through play, meaningful interactions, and with consistently modeled behaviors from you.

PLAY

- Older toddlers often start to enact or reenact whole series

of events they've witnessed or been engaged in themselves, but form another's perspective.

- Encourage pretend play and experimentation with
"becoming" the doctor who gave him a shot, or the
mama who put him to bed, or even the pet who wants to
be fed or walked.

Great Resource: **Learn With Less podcast episode, "Raising
Emotionally Intelligent Kids Through Play,"** featuring an interview with marriage and family therapist, Kelli McCarty

TALK

- Point out how a negative behavior affected another person, and visually identify behaviors that are linked to
actions

  - *"Oh, this little boy looks so sad that you took his toy.
    I wonder what we could do to help him feel better.
    Let's think for a second."*

- Walk your child through the ability to problem-solve in a
social situation.

SING

- Songs you can sing about your child's positive qualities
can make praise feel more playful.
- Adapting songs to your environment and circumstances
can be a simple way to do this

- For instance, *"The Wheels On The Bus Go Round and Round"* can become *"I love it when you give me a hug..."*

MOVE

- Place photographs or images of people with different expressions in different places in your home or around the room, and go on a scavenger hunt for them.

26 Months Old: Spatial Sense & Reasoning

Spatial Sense and Reasoning (Cognitive Development)

Your child's spatial sense is related to early mathematical concepts that relate to eventual geometrical learning. These are concepts relating to shape, size, space, position, direction, and movement.[8]

If we take into account the idea that young children learn through movement, activating their muscles and feeling their bodies moving in space, it should be clear that the most efficient way to teach concepts such as spatial and shape vocabulary are not going to be drilling and

---

8. Fromboluti, C. S., & Rinck, N. (1999 June). Early childhood: Where learning begins. U.S. Department of Education, Office of Educational Research and Improvement, National Institute on Early Childhood Development and Education. Retrieved on May 11, 2018 from https://www2.ed.gov/pubs/EarlyMath/title.htmloffsite link

practicing flashcards or pressing buttons on "learning toys" that make sounds and spout out words for shapes.

WHAT YOU CAN DO:

Integrate movement, add language. Use your body, your toddler's body, and a few other objects to explore and engage with, in your home or community. Use vocabulary in context and help your child make sense of her conceptual understanding by exposure and experience.

PLAY

- Hide smaller objects under, behind, on top, or inside of stacking blocks, nesting cups, and mixing bowls.
- Make a sensory bin full of objects of the same shape or the same size.
- Make use of items in the kitchen:

   ◦ Nesting bowls or measuring spoons (things that fit inside one another)
   ◦ Snack containers, which help your child problem-solve (find the matching lid!) and explore size and shape concepts by changing the position and direction

- Explore puzzles, or create them by cutting up paper or photographs into two halves or three pieces so your child can figure out how to put them back together.

TALK

- Talk about the way things relate to each other.
- Wonder aloud what your child is doing or what might

happen if she does it a different way.
- Let her know what she can do if she needs to ask for help.

SING

- Make up a song about where something might be hiding. When you find it, make a big deal of talking about where it was.
- Though the song's origins are questionable, you might borrow the format of the song *"10 Little Indians"* and adapt it to *"Where is the ___?"*

MOVE

- Place things inside of other objects, turn them over and stack them on top of each other.
- Explore objects that require more dextrous movements, such as:

  - Spinning (e.g., a salad spinner, a music box)
  - Twisting or ripping (e.g., stickers, tape)
  - Pouring (e.g., cups, funnels)
  - Finding the "exact fit" (e.g., tops on containers)

26 Months Old: Joint Attention & Directed Speech

Joint Attention and Directed Speech (Communicative Development)

We often form expectations around what our toddlers "should" be interested in within a particular activity or experience. Whether we're reading a bedtime story, spending a day at the museum, or paying to attend a music class, we want our children to be able to attend to the stimulus at hand. The trouble is, our toddlers often have their own ideas about what's interesting.

When we let go of the idea that we can control what our toddlers are interested in, and instead focus on creating interesting, novel, curiosity-inducing experiences for and around them, we create a true learning environment. Research into verbal language development indicates that a young child's communication develops more quickly when he is in control of topic selection in a social setting.[9]

In other words, your child pays better (and often, more focused, longer) attention to things in which he is interested, rather than things in which you think he should be interested. Your child might rather point out the star on a single page of a book (instead of sitting on your lap reading each page). The pebbles outside the doors to the museum's entrance may be infinitely interesting (instead of the inside of the museum itself). The coat closet door opening and closing may be much more interesting than the music class going on inside the room. In each of these examples, your child is communicating his interests to you. When we offer the language around that which our children are already interested, we provide a much more powerful opportunity for joint attention (the shared focus or attention of two "communication partners" upon an outside object). When your child engages in joint

9. Tomasello, M., & Farrar, M. (1986). Joint Attention and Early Language. Child Development, 57(6), 1454-1463. doi:10.2307/1130423

attentional acts, it is more likely that the vocal information you provide will be retained.[10]

WHAT YOU CAN DO:

Let go of your own expectations about what your child should be interested in – and play to his interests, instead.

PLAY

- Follow your child's interests, and remember that those moments are often the most powerful learning opportunities.

    - It can be difficult to let go of the notion that experiences in which we invest, or in which there is social pressure to engage in a particular way, are not actually developmentally appropriate.

TALK

- Talk in simple sentences about what it is your child is doing or interested in.
- Describe his actions, how the objects:

    - Look
    - Move
    - Feel

10. Goodwyn, S. W., & Acredolo, L. P. (1993). Symbolic gesture versus word: Is there a modality advantage for onset of symbol use? [Electronic version] Child Development, 688-701. From Academic Search Premier.

- Use gestures (e.g., point, wave, body action) as appropriate, to model various ways we all communicate, and to enhance your own communication with your child.

SING

- Take one word for the object or experience your child is exploring (e.g., "star" or "smooth")
  - Recall a song that already has that word (e.g., "Twinkle, Twinkle, Little Star")
  - Adapt an existing, familiar song to include that word or concept, and other things that are related (e.g., *"It's smooth, it's smooth... but this one is rough!"* to the tune of Ram, Sam, Sam)

MOVE

- Encourage exploration of your environment.
- Let your child know he is free to explore (safe) spaces... and when a space or object is not available, tell him why – and offer an alternative!
- If you have time or safety constraints to your child's exploration, let him know he has just "one more minute" before you remove him from his activity.

27 Months Old: Artistic Expression

Artistic Expression (Motor Development)

Many aspects of early literacy include exposure to and exploration and awareness of print. When we provide materials for creative expression, we provide them with a way to engage with the process of creation. You may have heard the term "process art," which essentially refers to the idea that the process is, developmentally, just as (if not more important than) the outcome. Providing process art experiences for your child goes hand-in-hand with "open-ended play," and creates an opportunity for exploration and problem-solving. It provides a rich, stimulating experience wherein your child can explore through her senses and with her body, experience cause and effect (quite literally, when she draws, paints, or attaches tape to paper), and experiment with concepts like color, texture, size, and length.[11]

Like all aspects of motor development, the act of drawing (eventually, forming the skills for both more "formal" creative expression and for writing) generally progresses within stages. First, we often see random scribbling, where a child is putting together the fact that their own movements result in marks on the paper, clay, or other surface. Next, we see more controlled scribbling, showing more control with tools. Toddlers often make repetitive marks on the page, and begin to hold the writing instrument with a few fingers (rather than the earlier, less refined fist). The next stage is marked by more lines, various shapes, and patterns.[12] Just as verbal output is becoming imitative, so are the beginnings of writing output – and while your child may not be writing letters, the emerging skills to create those letters and other shapes are starting to appear. Your child may draw a picture that is representative of an object, person, place, or experience in her life. This is a perfect example of the interconnectedness of early learning, in that a child

11. Farrell-Kirk, R. (2007 February). Tips on understanding and encouraging your child's artistic development. June 10, 2008.
12. Queensland School Curriculum Council. (1998). Supporting your child's writing development.

must be motorically able to draw a representation of an object as well as verbally express that thought to another person so that it can be communicated.

WHAT YOU CAN DO:

Create experiences for your child to engage with artistic and creative materials in and around your home. Creation can come in the form of building (e.g., blocks), mixing materials and textures together, as well as the more traditional ideas with paper.

PLAY

- Provide safely supervised access to a variety of materials for creation, patterning, coloring, taping, or painting.
- Think about all the different modes of artistic expression (e.g., sculpture, painting, drawing) when considering possibilities, as well as various parts of the color spectrum (e.g., neutrals, greyscale, rainbow).
- Materials may come from:

  - The art store
  - The recycling bin (e.g., bubble wrap, paper towel rolls, egg cartons)
  - Your other play materials (e.g., blocks, play doh, or colorful pureed fruits)

Great Resource: **Learn With Less podcast episode, Pairing Process Art and Early Literacy Experiences,** featuring KidArtLit co-founder and arts educator, Julia Lindsteadt

TALK

- Talk about what your child is doing, or what she did.

- Talk about the shapes she made, the colors she used, the objects she drew, the size of the pieces she's using (or ripping) – or make something alongside her, and talk about what you're creating!

[NOTE: this is not about your level of skill or proficiency! This is about going through the process with her!]

SING

- Many of us enjoy listening to music in the background as we create – see what feels inspirational for your child!
- Alternatively, remember that creating music together is a wonderfully artistic expression in and of itself, and involves reactions from others, turn-taking, and movement.

MOVE

- Art and creativity can help a child regulate their emotions when they are experiencing big feelings.
- The act of squeezing play dough or creating strong marks on a page may be enough to help your child feel better, and can also create a venue for her to "show" you how she is feeling.

27 Months Old: Happiness and

Relationships

Happiness and Relationships (Social/Emotional Development)

In a study that famously set out to predict the most influential factors in a person's overall happiness, the lead investigator was quoted as having learned that "the only thing that really matters in life are your relationships to other people."[13] In study after study, developmental research indicates that the single most important factor in a young child's life (as a predictor of overall success, academic ability, capacity to regulate one's emotions and form and maintain healthy relationships) is a warm and positive relationship with a caregiver.

We all do our best as parents and caregivers. We can't be there all the time. We all struggle to juggle and manage the duties of life and our relationships with our children and adult partnerships. All we can do is our best, which is to create as many moments with our little ones to make it perfectly clear to them that they are valued, respected, loved, and cherished.

Again, the most important factor in your little one's development is that warm, positive relationship with a caregiver. Whether your child is at home with you or another caregiver, or at a day care facility with other caregivers and peers, this positive relationship is about having a caregiver who models positive face-to-face interactions, who is responsive, who is present, and who creates a safe environment for exploration. This is what allows a young child to learn to trust the world around him, feel secure in his attachment to one or more other human beings, and confidently learn to explore the world around him. This is how he learns.

Positive modeling, positive self-image, and positive relationships are the basis for a child's ability to form successful relationships, succeed academically (and otherwise), and build the tools to work through con-

13. Vaillant, G. E. (2002). Aging well: Surprising guideposts to a happier life from the landmark Harvard study of adult development. Boston, MA: Little, Brown.

flict and discord throughout the lifespan. This is the job of parent and caregiver: to provide this for our little ones.

WHAT YOU CAN DO:

Allow your child time for independent play, but remember he may want you to be present even when you're not playing "together." His exploration paired with his need for your presence is part of what allows him to form his own identity within the world.

PLAY

- During those times that you're together, make the most of routine and ritual, creating social and play routines out of otherwise potentially mundane moments.
  - Use a diaper wipe to play peekaboo during a diaper change
  - Keep interesting objects in the bathtub (the perfect time for "water play")
  - Offer objects for scooping, squeezing, pouring, measuring, etc (these can easily be repurposed objects found in the kitchen)

TALK

- Try to stay present within interactions, as much as possible.
- Try to create time in your day for multi-tasking, and time in your day for engaging with and/or involving your child in your tasks.
- Talk about what you're doing, and if it's not safe for your child to be involved, try to give him an age-appropriate

alternative

- If you're taking a hot plate out of the oven, give him a hot mitt to put on his hand, as well, and allow him to take a plate out of a cabinet, instead

SING

- Add music to your routines, and especially to your transitions between activities.
- A song can become a signal between you, marking the start of an activity (e.g., getting ready to make dinner, or a dance party).

Great Resource: **Learn With Less podcast episode, "Happiness and Relationships"**

MOVE

- Make music together, with the objects at hand.
- Take turns with your bodies and mouths creating different sounds and movements.

28 Months Old: Conceptual Learning

Conceptual Learning (Cognitive Development)

Young children learn new concepts best through experience – both direct and active (e.g., playing with and exploring objects and ideas in the world) as well as more passively (e.g., listening, observing an adult or peer's model). It's the combination of these two types of input that creates the ideal learning environment.[14]

When a child learns about a concept, we often think of learning about categorical information (for instance, "animal," "furniture," "vehicle"), but we often also associate them with properties ("hot," "blue"), directionality ("up," "in"), actions or events ("walking," "turning"), or states of being ("wet," "dry"), people or animals ("Mama," "Pup-pup"), and abstract ideas ("being good"). A child must also associate the word with its meaning to be able to understand and experiment with any particular concept.

WHAT YOU CAN DO:

Play games with opposites, and create opportunities for your child to experience concepts by highlighting words in the environment.

PLAY

- Within play and other regular routines, consider offering choices:

  ◦ Between two categories (e.g., "do you want to draw or build?")
  ◦ Within one category (e.g., "who should sing the song next, the lion or the elephant?")
  ◦ Between two "opposite" concept words (e.g., "want to pour cold water or warm water?")

- You not only provide access to these words and concepts within the environment, but you also give your child a

14. Gelman S. A. (2009). Learning from others: children's construction of concepts. Annual review of psychology, 60, 115-40.

sense of control and ownership over the situation.

TALK

- Talk about what you're doing as you're doing it, and what your child is doing as she's doing it.

  - If you're zipping a zipper, say the words out loud – "zip up! Zip down!"
  - If you capture your child's attention, repeat it.
  - Give her a turn, and say the words while she does it, as well.

SING

- Help solidify concepts by adapting words of a song to become opposite concept words (big and small, fast and slow, up and down) while acting these words out.

  - A prime example is replacing words of the song, "Open, Shut Them."

- Within a musical context, you're:

  - Creating a multi sensory context for learning (visual, auditory, proprioceptive, vestibular, etc)
  - Activating multiple parts of the brain while working within the framework of a melody (which is a repeated sequence of notes within a known rhythmic pattern)

MOVE

- Play games with opposites.
- Perform actions quickly and then slowly, go on top of something and then under, forward then backward.
- Try to use your own bodies in addition to objects you can manipulate.

28 Months Old: Sounds and Words

Sounds and Words (Communicative Development)

Phonemic awareness is a term that describes the ability to detect, identify, and use different speech sounds. The words "chat" and "pat" differ by one phoneme (speech sound): *ch* vs *p*. The ability to distinguish different sounds is linked to the development of emerging literacy skills in a young child.[15]

When we engage in rhyming activities, we can naturally support our children's phonemic awareness skills. In addition, we're naturally playing with language, and encouraging our children to do the same.

We know that children thrive on repetition; however, when we add a variable – a small change in the pattern with which they're familiar – that's where we really find the "gold." When we play with words, through music or in reading activities, it provides our children with more opportunities to process the sounds and patterns. When we change one small element – the words, the rhythm, or the motion, we do so within an already familiar context. This highlights different

15. Linnea C. Ehri, Simone R. Nunes, Dale M. Willows, Barbara Valeska Schuster, Zohreh Yaghoub-Zadeh and Timothy Shanahan, Reading Research Quarterly, Vol. 36, No. 3 (Jul. - Aug. - Sep., 2001), pp. 250-287

aspects or elements of an experience. In this way, your little one's brain is working to integrate and distinguish the familiar from the unfamiliar. In addition, the more you play with words, language, and your voice, the more likely it is that your child will, as well.

WHAT YOU CAN DO:

Perform finger plays and songs together, and read books with rhyming words or phrases.

PLAY

- The playful, flexible nature of language within songs or rhymes helps us as adults to focus on the interaction, and can help us get back in touch with that playful part of us from which our young children benefit so much.
- Vocal play – letting go of what something is "supposed" to sound like or what the words to a song are "supposed" to be, is absolutely a form of play!

TALK

- We don't always remember the words to even "familiar" nursery rhymes, so don't be afraid to play with language and get creative!
- Take a nursery rhyme (or a picture that reminds you of a song or nursery rhyme) and play with the words in it.
- Go through a book, magazine, or coupon mailer and point at objects, then think of words that rhyme with those objects, and make a silly sentence.

  - For instance, if you find a dress, you might say something like:

- *"She's eating in her dress – oh please don't make a mess!"*
- *"That cow says 'moo!' But he doesn't wear a shoe!"*

SING

- Take all the words out of a song and hum the song, sing only on "la" or replace all the words with your child's name.
- Tap to the rhythm without the tune, make up an entirely new verse with your own rhyming words.

MOVE

- Take a walk around your home or in your community (e.g., on a walk, in the grocery store, at the library) and point out interesting things along the way.
- Make up silly songs about them, or look at them in new ways (for instance, upside down).

  - In fact, you can sing a song about something you find "around town" and what it looks like "upside down!"

29 Months Old: Indoor – Outdoor

Indoor – Outdoor (Motor Development)

Provision of a variety of experiences for movement and environmental exploration is the basis for your child's ability to learn about the world. Over the last few decades especially, Western society has come to value academic learning, often holding it above all else. The trouble we face is that in order to develop the brain, we must provide ways to develop the body.

Our homes are full of places and objects to explore. Most of the daily routines in which we engage are inside various spaces of our homes, and our children learn to use each space in the "appropriate" manner (e.g., we bathe or use the toilet in the bathroom, we make food in the kitchen, we sleep in the bedroom). By now, you've found new ways to allow your child to explore everyday household objects to support the development of symbolic play and pretend play.

Open-ended materials for play are the hallmark of exploration and learning. Your child may come back to these objects in new ways over time, and we know that repetition with variation – a variety of texture, of type, of material, of size, shape and other properties – is the key to the expansion of learning. Materials inside the home are wonderful, but giving the opportunity to explore materials outside of the home is also essential. As we've discussed before, the outdoor environment offers other unique kinds of materials (such as sticks, flowers, leaves, dirt, rocks), and affords opportunities for play in every way.

Your child is using her brain and body to detect patterns, explore the mechanics of materials at hand (how they work, what parts are involved in a whole, how things move and can be manipulated), and sense how her body works in relation to her environment.

WHAT YOU CAN DO:

Find opportunities to explore both inside and outside, and with a variety of materials.

PLAY

- Find opportunities to problem-solve with large or heavy objects.
- Collaborate with your child (or find opportunities for your child and other peers to collaborate) to complete a task.
- Build in turn-taking opportunities with tools or projects.

Great Resource: **Learn With Less podcast episode, "The Power of Play Through Movement"** with physical therapist and founder of Move Play Grow, Wendi McKenna

TALK

- Discuss what equipment you both might need before you go outside

    - We need shoes
    - If it's cold, you'll need another layer
    - If you're going to play with water, you'll need to be waterproof / naked / have an extra change of clothes handy

- Talk about what you see, what you feel, how much pressure something needs to be moved.
- Model the act of asking for help, and encourage your child to do the same by being watchful if she is frustrated.

    - You might let her know your expectations in advance (e.g., *"That looks difficult. You'll let me know if you need me. You can always say, 'help, please!'"*)

SING

- Engage in song and rhythm activities both inside and out.
- Find percussive instruments in a variety of objects, such as sticks, water, metal grates, leaves.

MOVE

- Go on a hunt for shapes, colors, animals, vehicles, rocks, or any other category of objects in which your child might hold an interest.
- Take extra time to walk down the sidewalk or give your child the chance to explore a new pathway.

29 Months Old: Emotional Regulation

Emotional Regulation (Social/Emotional)

Our emotional responses are, essentially, physical, neurological, and biochemical reactions to situations and stimuli presented from outside our bodies. This includes bodily processes like heart rate, blood flow, respiration, and more. Our ability to self-regulate has to do with the maturation of our brains; for instance, throughout infancy and toddlerhood, the frontal lobe of the brain is developing rapidly. This area of the brain is involved in the ability to regulate emotions and perform what's known as "executive functioning" skills (consider the skills an "executive" needs to perform – the ability to plan, behave appropriately in social situations, solve problems, etc) – all areas with which your toddler likely struggles.

We also know that emotional responses are part of temperament and behavior. We can think of the ways emotions are expressed through actions: when your young child cries, laughs, or withdraws from an activity, she is communicating a behavioral response of some kind.

Finally, emotional responses are linked inextricably to our cognitive abilities. For a young child to be able to participate in or complete a task (whether that is in the context of play, participating in a meal, or participating in another caregiving or daily routine of some kind), she must be able to attend to what she's doing. She needs to be able to problem-solve a way to get what she wants or needs if she is feeling hungry, tired, frustrated, or dissatisfied, and she needs the language to express that feeling to those around her.

That's where we come in. These three areas (the physical, behavioral, and cognitive aspects) are all involved in the development of emotional regulation. As humans, we're not born with the ability to regulate our emotions (just like we're not born able to walk or speak), and our ability to self-regulate fluctuates and responds to outside forces (how tired we are, how hungry we are, etc). Your child learns through imitation, practice, and observation, how to get her needs met. Like anything else, this takes time, and is influenced by responsive caregiving. That's why it's so important for us as parents and caregivers to be as consistent as possible in our own responses: so we can positively model and shape the ways our infants and toddlers respond to their environment.[16]

In order to help your young child scaffold his skills, you must bridge the gap between what you want him to be able to do, and what he can currently do. Provide the developmentally appropriate level of support and managing your own expectations of your young child's ability to use appropriate emotional responses. Calm your child when he's frustrated, end an activity or make it easier, provide the tools to express himself through language, and muster up as much patience and grace as you can – for both your child's behavior and your own. In so doing, you allow your child to build confidence and eventually build the skills

16. Florez, I.R. (2011). Developing Young Children's Self-Regulation through Everyday Experiences: Young Children, v66 n4 p46-51 Jul 2011.

necessary to independently begin to regulate his emotions. Keep in mind that you're building pathways in the brain, which takes time and requires heavy lifting and lots of practice (both in quantity and quality) from you in order to effectively support your child toward independence.[17]

WHAT YOU CAN DO:

Respond to your child's needs by allowing him to understand he can rely on you to provide what's necessary for him to succeed and feel supported.

PLAY

- Arrange your home or designated "play area" so that your child can access appropriate play materials as independently as possible.

  - At the same time, define limits within which both of you are comfortable.
  - This may require the provision of a bit of control on your child's part, meaning that if he wants something that is not safe or unavailable, you might find a way to offer a few versions of that activity or material that is available.

- Often, you may be able to satisfy your child's need if you can determine whether he needs to:

  - **Experience** what you're doing (e.g., peek inside the hot oven to see what you see, bang a hammer on the wood)

17. Bronson, M. (2000). Recognizing and Supporting the Development of Self-Regulation in Young Children. Young Children, 55(2), 32-37. Retrieved from http://www.jstor.org/stable/42727768

- **Take control** over something (e.g., imitating your movements – stirring the pot or sweeping the pathway)
- **Connect** with you (e.g., your attention is on another child, another adult, or another activity)

Great Resource: **Learn With Less podcast episode, Using The Language of Listening with Infants and Toddlers,** with author and journalist Tracy Cutchlow

TALK

- Respond to your young child, and make attempts to be interactive and attentive to signals in his routine that help him make sense of both routines as well as transitions between activities.

  - Acknowledge out loud what's coming next, either with words only, or with words and the addition of pictures, or objects.

- Acknowledge (and accept) your child's emotions, and provide coping skills so he can move through more difficult moments more effectively.
- Reflect back to your child what you think he might be feeling or simply what he's just done

  - This also applies if you're the one who "lost your cool!"

- Reflect back what you or your child is feeling or what happened, in just a few simple sentences:

  - *"You're/I'm feeling really sad. That hurt! Ouch! I saw*

*you fall down. Let's see, when I feel sad, I sometimes
need to take a break or get a hug. Do you think
either of those things would help?"*

Great Resource: **Learn With Less podcast episode, "Emotional Regulation in Young Children"**

SING

- Singing songs about the ways others feel provides vocabulary for emotions, models empathy, and provides possible solutions so you can help to guide your child through the experience to the other side.
- One of my personal favorites is an adaptation of the song, *"Where is Thumpkin"* that you can use to sing about different emotions you see in images – *"Where is a Sad / Happy / Excited Face."*

Great Resource: **Strength In Words: Music For Families** musical album

MOVE

- Use movement to imitate the feelings you're experiencing.
    - You might integrate this with a musical experience, channeling excitement, sadness, anger, or frustration into:

- A dance party
- A drum circle,
- A swaying/humming calm down lullaby

4. 30 - 36 Months

Within this chapter, I'll suggest additional resources for you to explore on the Learn With Less website. You can find all of those resources organized by chapter here: https://learnwithless.com/toddler-bonus

30 Months Old: Attention Expansion

Attention Expansion (Cognitive Development)

While it may be surprising, unstructured play helps to increase your child's attention span. When your child is able to manipulate objects in her own environment in her own way, with her own body, and with objects of her own choosing, she can perform experiments that she herself creates.[1] Active engagement with materials in the environment, or "focused attention," is the kind of play that encourages information processing, or what we often think of as "learning."[2] [3]

Though a child's ability to attend to any particular activity or task is related to her interest in the materials at hand, we also know that a child's attention skills develop within her environment and are influenced by social interactions.[4] Therefore, a child's adult counterparts strongly influence that child's exploration and play environment. Emo-

1. Bergen, D., Reid, R., and Torelli, L. (2009). Educating and Caring for Very Young Children: The Infant/Toddler Curriculum (2nd ed.). New York, NY: Teachers College Press.
2. Gaertner, B. M., Spinrad, T. L., & Eisenberg, N. (2008). Focused Attention in Toddlers: Measurement, Stability, and Relations to Negative Emotion and Parenting. Infant and child development, 17(4), 339-363.
3. Ruff HA, Lawson KR. Development of sustained, focused attention in young children during free play. Developmental Psychology. 1990;26:85–93.
4. Rothbart MK, Bates JE. Temperament. In: Damon W, Eisenberg N, editors. Handbook of child psychology: Vol. 3. Social, emotional and personality development. 5th ed. Wiley; New York: 1998. pp. 105–176.

tional support from the adult in the form of affirmations ("that's great! I like what you're doing!"), and a generally positive affect (positive response and attention from the adult) have been linked to higher levels of focused attention.[5][6][7] This suggests that an adult's presence (without structuring or directing play) can actually increase your child's attention span. Though this may seem antithetical, your presence *does* support and promote more independent – and longer periods of – play over time.

Lastly, research suggests that parents and caregivers who are aware of their child's cues within a play context (rather than attempting to control and interfere with their child's interests) are more likely to create an environment wherein their child learns to complete tasks, stay motivated, and use positive self-regulation strategies.[8][9]

Important to note is what is considered a "typical" attention span for a toddler, and research suggests that, on average, a child of this age (between 2-3 years of age) can be attentive and engaged with any given toy or activity (e.g., reading, music, sensory experience) for up to 5-8 minutes. Within this focused attention span, she can also shift between her activity and an adult speaking, and reengage with what she was doing beforehand.[10]

5. Dunn J, Creps C, Brown J. Children's family relationships between two and five: Developmental changes and individual differences. Social Development. 1996;5:230–250.
6. Valiente, C., Eisenberg, N., Spinrad, T. L., Reiser, M., Cumberland, A., Losoya, S. H., & Liew, J. (2006). Relations among mothers' expressivity, children's effortful control, and their problem behaviors: A four-year longitudinal study. Emotion, 6(3), 459-472. http://dx.doi.org/10.1037/15283542.6.3.459
7. Gaertner, B. M., Spinrad, T. L., & Eisenberg, N. (2008). Focused Attention in Toddlers: Measurement, Stability, and Relations to Negative Emotion and Parenting. Infant and child development, 17(4), 339-363.
8. Grolnick WS. The psychology of parental control: How well-meaning parenting backfires. Guilford Press; New York: 2003.
9. Function and content of maternal demands: developmental significance of early demands for competent action. Kuczynski L, Kochanska G Child Dev. 1995 Jun; 66(3):616-28.
10. Mize, L. (2017). Let's Talk About Talking. Kentucky: teachmetotalk.com

WHAT YOU CAN DO:

Keep the environment interesting by making small variations, and use the time you're already spending near or with your child to engage with her purposefully.

PLAY

- Call attention to "novel" stimuli in the environment, and arrange a tableau with your child's play materials and/or with general household or natural objects.
- Vary the kinds of objects (e.g., consider texture and other properties) and the "plane" on which you offer them (above her, beside her, in front of her).

TALK

- Instead of guiding your child to perform a specific task with an object, talk about what she is doing and what she's looking at, or explain how the object works (and/or what it does).
- Make comments about the similarities or differences between what she's working with and other objects around her.
- Make positive comments about her actions, and encourage her to keep doing what she's doing.

SING

- Allow your child's actions to guide an activity, looking for and honoring her communicative acts (such as gestures, facial expressions, vocalizations, verbalizations).
- Provide a rhythmic or musical experience with something she's manipulating by placing that word within a rhyme.

MOVE

- Move cushions around furniture, place them on the floor in a line, or create tunnels, and encourage your child to interact with them in new ways

  ° Building a tower
  ° Hopping on them
  ° Falling forward onto them
  ° Moving under them

- Comment on what she is doing, suggest new ways to move, and comment on her creativity when she arranges them in a new way.

30 Months Old: Sabotage

Sabotage (Communicative Development)

We all want to encourage our children to develop independent problem-solving skills. In order to do this within a context of communication, many therapists utilize a strategy called "sabotage" to help tempt a child to communicate (without being manipulative or forced). Essentially, the adult creates a situation wherein the child must communicate to solve a problem by obstructing the child's path in some way.

Since you are purposefully creating a situation wherein your little one has to solve a problem, it becomes very important that you provide "just enough" support so that your child does not become too frustrated.

As we've discussed in previous modules, young children are constantly making assessments about whether something is mildly frustrating or so difficult that it's not even worth attempting. We must cultivate expectations that are within their reach, but at a slightly higher level than where they're comfortable. We want to "scaffold" their ability to obtain the desired result by creating a little boost for them to get to the next step up. We don't want that next step to seem too far away, but we want to expect slightly more than they're currently able to do.[11] We place small challenges in front of them to *assist* in their learning, and to create *new* opportunities for them. In other words, we must create a fun and positive challenge. Putting your proverbial foot down and creating a situation wherein your child *must* perform "or else" will undoubtedly result in a misguided attempt to use this strategy. What you're doing is creating a communication *temptation*: you are *tempting* your child to do something – not forcing him.

There are many ways to set up the opportunity to gently sabotage your toddler to encourage him to initiate communication. A key ingredient for this strategy to work is to use a factor of silliness. Reacting with humor, and keeping the connection between you strong, facilitates trust and helps your child learn there will be someone to gently guide him along the way as he becomes independent and self-sufficient.[12]

WHAT YOU CAN DO:

Within familiar routines or materials, purposefully forget a step or withhold an essential piece.

11. Bowen, C. (2011). Supporting speech and language progress in children with CAS or sCAS. Retrieved from http://www.speech-language-therapy.com/on June 24, 2016.
12. Mize, L. (2008). A Little Frustration CAN Go A Long Way... Using Sabotage and Witholding Effectively to Entice Your Toddler To Talk. Retrieved from http://www.teachmetotalk.com/on June 22, 2016.

PLAY

- Use objects to help you "play dumb."
- Place favorite play materials inside a clear box or container, or just out of reach.

TALK

- Encourage small steps toward new skills.

  - If your child has never used a pointing gesture, this is what you can work toward (by modeling that gesture in many activities or in interactions you have, and then as a suggestion that this is what you expect from him).
  - If your child has never said the word, "open," but is starting to use words or imitate the first sound of a word, work towards that!
  - If your child is using multiple-word utterances, but you're trying to encourage him to ask you vs demand from you, model the act of asking questions!

SING

- Hum or sing a tune while you wait for your child to let you know he needs something from you.

Great Resource: **Learn With Less podcast episode, "The Art of Sabotage"**

MOVE

- Provide objects within containers you know your child may not be able to open independently, or that are just out of her reach.
- Provide a lid to a container that is purposefully the wrong size.

31 Months Old: Messy Play

Messy Play (Motor Development)

Young children learn through movement and touch, and from the beginning, interact with others by way of observation and imitation. As children become more mobile, they become more able to try new things through practice and experience. We know infants and toddlers learn holistically and experientially, and we've spoken about the way open-ended play materials and activities are often very powerful for learning. One important area of open-ended play is known as "messy play," which some parents and caregivers tend to shy away from, as it can present a more committed challenge when it comes to time and energy with regard to set up and clean up.

Messy play *can* be a big ordeal, the kind that conjures up images of walls and floors spattered with paint, extra loads of laundry, and a lot of extra work... but it doesn't have to be. When we give our young children opportunities to explore textures, whether bumpy and smooth or wet and dry, we provide them with opportunities to learn. When a young child can play with materials that allow her to explore the environment with all her senses, this is holistic learning. What we refer to as "messy play" is often simply what happens when a child is able to engage in rich textural experiences. When your child is able to freely explore the world of texture, she learns the concepts of slimy, smooth, wet, bumpy, etc. She learns that what she does with her body has an impact on the objects with which she plays, and on the world (cause and effect). She learns about vocabulary when you talk about what she, or the two of you, are doing. Since this kind of play is naturally open-ended, she learns about self-expression and creation. She learns about what it is to investigate and problem-solve when she manipulates materials.

So, how do we provide these experiences in a way that we as adults are also comfortable? We must bring a bit of forethought to the ways in which we can structure the activity so that we're "ok" with the kind of clean up that will need to happen at the end (and, given a toddler's short attention span, the end of a very messy experience might come more quickly than we feel is "worth" the experience). We must remember to balance our own judgments and values with those experiences of our children. We find ways to incorporate wipeable or hose-able surfaces, safe tools, and we provide supervision. We can even involve our young children (again, at their own level, whenever possible) with the clean up – creating a separate activity out of that! Most importantly, within the context of messy play experiences, we must remember that the value lies in the exploration rather than "getting the job done."

WHAT YOU CAN DO:

Find ways to incorporate messy play opportunities into your everyday routines or within short play opportunities, and utilize simple clean up hacks by pre-thinking the environment or materials needed.

PLAY

- Food as an opportunity for messy play is a simple way to start.
  - Offer brightly colored purees or colorful tea bags for painting on paper or on one's own body.
- Using food as paint has the added benefit of potentially easing any anxiety or unease with solids.

- Should your child be averse to touching the "paint," you can always place it inside a clear plastic bag.

Great Resource: **Learn With Less podcast episode, "What's So Great About Messy Play?"**

TALK

- Talk through the activity, providing words for the perceptual motor experience your child is having.
- Wonder aloud about what she might do next.
- State what she is doing, how she's moving and using the materials.

SING

- Sing about what you are doing and what your child is doing.
  - A tune I like to use is, *"Put Your Finger In The Air,"* which you can easily adapt the words to what is happening in your environment.

MOVE

- Provide opportunities to place objects inside other

objects, or to practice fine motor skills.

- ○ Use a colander and a mix of cooked spaghetti and uncooked spaghetti to explore texture and property.
- ○ Use differently sized bowls to pour, scoop, and transfer water.

31 Months Old: Theory Of Mind & Emotional Language

Theory of Mind and Emotional Language (Social/Emotional Development)

We've discussed parts of social cognition, in that imitation, sharing, testing behaviors, empathy, and pretend play are all skills and abilities that take time and develop over time, layer upon layer. They are all also part of the development of "theory of mind," or the ability to take another person's perspective, and understand that not everyone shares the same thoughts, ideas, and feelings in the same moment. There is a fairly clear progression of abilities that help a child to form their emerging understanding of theory of mind (the basis for which, again, develops over time over the first five years of life).

One such skill is the ability to recognize and talk about emotions, and to use emotional language to describe what our children and others around us are feeling (whether that's positive, negative, or associated with specific needs such as food, drink, or sleep). Using emotional language builds your young child's abilities to identify his own emotions, eventually building skills to regulate those emotions. It also helps him learn to recognize that other people may feel differently than he does at a particular moment. This also relates to understanding the causes and consequences of actions and emotions.

When we label emotions – of people in the environment (especially when strong emotions are witnessed), those your child expresses, or those you're experiencing, you give words to feelings and reassure your child that feelings of all kinds are valued and accepted. If you explain the way actions make people feel, or make predictions about why people might feel a certain way, you work on sensitizing your young child to an important part of social language, cognition, and perspective taking, naturally and fluidly.

WHAT YOU CAN DO:

Acknowledge all emotions, positive and negative, and provide the vocabulary for them. Often, validating your child's emotions (or your own!) helps to begin to diffuse an emotionally charged situation and pave the way forward.

PLAY

- Using images in books, magazines, photographs, printed pictures, or elsewhere in the environment (e.g., bus stop, billboard, store window), take a moment to observe:

  - How people look (e.g., physical attributes like long or short hair, types of clothing they're wearing)
  - What they're doing (e.g., standing, sitting, reading, praying, talking, laughing, crying, sleeping)
  - How they might be feeling (e.g., tired, happy, bored)

TALK

- Acknowledge what you're feeling when you "lose your cool," by:

- Taking a deep breath and simply stating how you're feeling and why (keep it short and sweet – *"I'm feeling frustrated because when I hear you whining, it hurts my ears... let's both try to use a different voice."*

- Acknowledge how your child is feeling when he loses his cool (regardless of whether you think it's a valid frustration)!

SING

- Sing songs or perform finger plays about feelings, utilizing a visual support
  - An image/photograph
  - An object (like a puppet)
  - Your fingers themselves

Great Resource: **Learn With Less podcast episode, "A Theory Of The Mind"**

MOVE

- Provide the physical space for your child to have big feelings.
- If your child screeches or screams, try to find a way for him to get that feeling "out" in a socially acceptable manner
  - For instance, by allowing him to remove himself

from a social area of the home (and instead going into a bedroom or outside) to fulfill that need to scream.
- ° Try not to make negative "judgments" about the big emotion, but simply keep it about *finding an acceptable solution*

32 Months Old: Treasure Collectors

Treasure Collectors (Cognitive Development)

Your child may be intrigued by particular objects she finds in your home or community. She may collect a particular type of object, such as pebbles, leaves, or flowers, and insist upon saving or storing them.

This "collecting" of treasures is a way for her to exert her independence, and to create a physical representation of her space and interests. It also supports her ability to classify objects, compare and contrast (and build upon relationships between objects), and add to her knowledge of the world through experience and engaging with her environment.[13]

WHAT YOU CAN DO:

Support her interests by providing places in which she can collect and store treasures, and engage regularly in treasure hunting excursions.

13. California Department of Education, California Infant/Toddler Learning & Development Foundations. Sacramento: California Department of Education Press, 2009.

PLAY

- Create physical space in your home that is designated for treasure collection, such as a special box, basket, or shelf.
- Help your child take pride in her own collection by providing pockets or space in a bag on your journey.

TALK

- Provide time to discuss the objects your child has collected.

  ○ Relate them to other objects and other experiences (other items in the collection or in the home, images in books or stories you've read).

- Play with the objects by:

  ○ Hiding them
  ○ Sorting them
  ○ Including them in pretend play

SING

- Make music or musical instruments with the treasures themselves (e.g., place pebbles in an enclosed snack container)
- Sing a song about the various objects.

  ○ You might adapt a familiar song such as *"Mary Had*

A Little Lamb" to be about your child's name and the objects she has.

MOVE

- Create a regular routine or ritual of treasure hunting in your community, especially outdoors:

  - In a neighborhood
  - In a backyard
  - In a park

32 Months Old: Environmental Print

Environmental Print (Communicative Development)

When we think of "early literacy," often the first activity that comes to mind is sitting together reading a book with your child... but early literacy experiences are everywhere. The basis for the skills that will eventually make your child into a reader includes various skills such as phonological awareness (or, the awareness of the sounds within words); print awareness and interest in print (the understanding that print objects have symbolic meaning, the general sense of how to handle a book – e.g., page turning); letter knowledge (knowing and recognizing various letters and the sounds they represent); and possession of a varied vocabulary (understanding the meaning of words).

As you well know, sitting down to read with your toddler is not always practical or possible. However, there are many ways to integrate early literacy experiences and routines into your daily life with an active toddler. Research suggests that many children lack exposure to environments that promote early and emergent literacy.[14] The fact is, for busy toddlers, there's no sense in putting unnecessary pressure on yourself as a caregiver. There will be some days when your toddler may enjoy sitting and being read to, and other days when we can bring early literacy experiences to them... or simply open our eyes to those around us.

Print awareness and letter knowledge don't require "drill and practice" flashcards. Print is everywhere in our homes (e.g., on food cans or boxes, packaging of any kind, books, coupon mailers, and magazines) and communities (e.g., grocery stores, bathrooms, bus stops, stop signs). Helping your child associate icons and images with symbolic language (e.g., a stop sign means "stop," a wheelchair parking spot indicates a place for someone who needs to be closer to the building) reinforces and solidifies print awareness and symbols, which, in turn, supports the development of various areas of language and communication.

WHAT YOU CAN DO:

Find print in your environment on walks or in your home, and implement time for "early literacy routines" (whether or not those include sitting and reading a book!)

PLAY

- Grab your coupon mailer and cut or tear out images of foods that look fun, or find matching images.

  ◦ Turn them over to play memory games
  ◦ Pretend to feed them to stuffed animals or other inanimate objects

- Write out the names for objects in your environment and

---

14. Lawhon, T. & Cobb, J.B. Early Childhood Education Journal (2002) 30: 113. https://doi.org/10.1023/A:1021253319248

place the labels where they're stored

- ◦ e.g., attach a card with the word "BLOCKS" to a box of blocks
- ◦ Add a photograph of the toy to the label if you're feeling extra fancy, to enhance the visual and provide an added way for your child to refer to his toys or to visually attend to the print next to the picture.

Great Resource: **Learn With Less Podcast Episode, "Playing With Purpose,"** featuring an interview with pediatric speech-language pathologist Emily Cohen of Tandem Speech.

TALK

- Take a look at what's around you, and comment on it!

  - ◦ Each time you walk up to a stop sign (or pass one in your car), point it out to your child.

- Read instructions or recipes aloud and alongside your child when you can, then follow those instructions in real life so your child can see and be part of the process of what it looks like to go from reading words on a page into participating in or completing a real life experience.

SING

- Sing songs about the images you see around you, the pictures in a book, or along with a book.

- Find a series of images (from magazines or printed from a web search) and sing a song about them.
- Find body part pictures for *"Head, Shoulders, Knees & Toes"* or animals for *"Old MacDonald Had a Farm."*

MOVE

- Find or create letters in your environment, out of sticks, leaves, or other natural objects.
- Paint or draw using writing tools (e.g., finger paint, chalk, crayons) inside or outside.
- Go on a scavenger hunt to find an "X" or other letters (hidden in the room under or inside other objects, or hanging on the wall.

Great Resource: **Learn With Less podcast episode, "How to Provide Early Literacy Experiences for Infants and Toddlers,"** featuring an interview with early interventionist, Kayla O'Neill, of Parenting Expert to Mom

33 Months Old: Rough and Tumble Play

Rough and Tumble Play (Motor Development)

As your child experiments more with the way his body moves and the ways in which he can use it in a social context, he will likely explore a wide range of movement. At times, he may display the need for a more vigorous play with his body and others (with you, other caregivers, and with peers). Rough and Tumble play has been studied for decades, and is present in young children from all over the world (as well as in many animals!), and research suggests that children use their bodies in this way in order to explore and practice complex social interactions.[15]

Though "big body" or "Rough and Tumble" play is often discouraged in Western society because it can resemble real fighting, there are distinct characteristics of which adults can be aware to differentiate the two, and to help children navigate the positive aspects of it. Rough and Tumble play adheres to the functions of all other types of play, meaning that it is enjoyable for all involved, there is no outward goal (other than the pursuit of joy), it occurs spontaneously and voluntarily, and it involves active, positive engagement by all participants[1617] Real fighting is characterized by the desire to inflict or threaten pain, and includes tense muscles and closed fists (rather than an open palm).[18]

WHAT YOU CAN DO:

Engage in big body play with your child. Model acceptable behavior, providing vocabulary when and if the play goes "too far." Set expectations and be consistent with your responses.

PLAY

- Support your child's exploration of Rough and Tumble play by clarifying expectations when necessary, but making attempts to intervene less when possible.
- Engaging in big body play with other peers and adults can help children build social skills.

15. Pellegrini, A., and Smith, Peter K. (1998). Physical activity play: The nature and function of a neglected aspect of play. Child Development, 69, 557-598.
16. Garvey, C. 1977. Play. Cambridge. MA: Harvard University Press, pg 10
17. Carlson, F. M. (2011). Rough Play: One of the Most Challenging Behaviors. Young Children.
18. Fry, D. 2005. "Rough-and-Tumble Social Play in Humans." In The Nature of Play: Great Apes and Humans, eds A.D. Pellegrini & P.K. Smith, 54-85. New York: Guilford Press.

- This might take the form of:

  - Dancing
  - Climbing
  - Jumping
  - Tickling

- It may or may not include equipment

  - Taking turns sliding down a couch pillow
  - Navigating a large ball

PLAY

- Take the opportunity to provide verbal feedback about what someone's body is "saying."

  - Point out what your body or face says when your child is playing, or what another child's body is telling your child.

- Rough and Tumble play is a natural opportunity to call attention to your child's development of empathy and perspective taking, as well as turn taking and cooperation.

SING

- Use music to:

  - Heighten your child's excitement level (using an

upbeat play song)
- ○ Lower and bring down the experience (using more of a melody)

- · Mirror the type of movement you want to encourage with the pace and loudness of the song (either your singing, or recorded music).

MOVE

- · Create opportunities to challenge balance, direction, and rotation, utilizing all planes of movement.
- · Think about actions like swinging, lifting, bouncing, spinning:

    - ○ Using just your own bodies (big body social routines such as "airplane" or "elevator")
    - ○ Including a large piece of fabric within which you can swing, drag, hide...

Great Resource: **Learn With Less podcast episode "Understanding Babies Through Movement,"** featuring an interview with somatic movement educator, Ania Witkowska

33 Months Old: Impulse Control

Impulse Control (Social/Emotional Development)

A big part of a person's temperament has to do with how much control that individual has over his or her own behavioral and emotional responses. Some of the areas pertaining to the management of our impulses include the ability to manage our attention (where and on what we focus), inhibit desires or needs (when they are not appropriate or desired by others), and activate a behavioral response to adapt to outside environmental forces. This ability to focus, adapt, and respond to one's environment is what people describe as the ability to "self-reg-ulate."[19][20]

In the first five years of life, a child's ability to purposefully or "effortfully" control emotional and behavioral responses is developing rapidly alongside other areas of learning. There is a great deal of variability in the rate of the emergence of this ability. Research shows that there is both a genetic predisposition for the development [21][22] as well as a strong environmental influence. Therefore, it *is* within your capacity as parent/caregiver to help your child develop the underlying skills.

There is a strong, positive correlation between a child's ability to control her impulses and that child's caregivers exhibiting a supportive, non-directive, less controlling/authoritative caregiving style.[23][24][25] Therefore, research suggests that the more actively we can support our children

19. Eisenberg, Nancy. (2005). Temperamental Effortful Control (Self-Regulation).
20. Kopp CB, Neufeld SJ. Emotional development during infancy. In: Davidson RJ, Scherer KR, Goldsmith HH, eds. Handbook of affective sciences. Oxford, United Kingdom: Oxford University Press; 2003:347-374.
21. Goldsmith HH, Buss KA, Lemery KS. Toddler and childhood temperament: Expanded content, stronger genetic evidence, new evidence for the impor-tance of environment. Developmental Psychology 1997;33(6):891-905.
22. Kochanska, G., Murray, K. T., & Harlan, E. T. (2000, Mar). Effortful control in early childhood: Continuity and change, antecedents, and implications for social development. Developmental Psychology, 36(2), 220-232.
23. Calkins SD, Smith CL, Gill KL, Johnson MC. Maternal interactive style across con-texts: Relations to emotional, behavioural, and physiological regulation during toddlerhood. Social Development 1998;7(3):350-369.
24. Gilliom M, Shaw DS, Beck JE, Schonberg MA, Lukon JL. Anger regulation in dis-advantaged preschool boys: Strategies, antecedents, and the development of self-control. Developmental Psychology 2002;38(2):222-235.
25. Olson SL, Bates JE, Bayles K. Early antecedents of childhood impulsivity: The role of parent-child interaction, cognitive competence, and temperament. Jour-nal of Abnormal Child Psychology 1990;18(3):317-334.

to make good choices, to accept and validate their feelings so they can feel confident to move forward, and to provide them with acceptable ways to do things independently, the more we will be supporting their abilities to control their impulses, and to develop skills related to self-regulation and executive functioning.

WHAT YOU CAN DO:

Validate your child's feelings, attempt to determine her underlying desire or goal, and redirect your child's need into an acceptable alternative activity.

PLAY

- Many toddlers around this age have a strong desire to complete tasks independently, but struggle to manage frustration or to accept assistance from a willing adult.
- Try scaffolding her needs: instead of offering to complete the task for her, point out one small way she might try it differently, ask if she'd like you to help her with one specific part of the task, or model the way you do it and then allow her to do it independently.
- Offer your child various safer or more acceptable ways to play with objects (or "like" objects)

  - Often, the need for independence is accompanied by a desire to be doing what you're doing.
  - For instance, cooking on a stove top may not be something with which your child can help you

- Alternatives exist, such as the creation of a cardboard box with drawn on burners so she can "pretend" to cook alongside you

  - Moving a high chair or standing on a stool so she can be at the same level as you
  - Giving her a job of her own – handing her the

wooden spoon so she can become "taste tester."

- If an acceptable alternative doesn't work, try taking turns or adapting activities to be safer or easier for your child.
- There may be moments during which your child simply must wait for you to finish what you are doing so that you can all be safe together.

  - Acknowledge her feelings and find something to do together once you're done.

TALK

- There may be moments wherein your child interrupts your conversations with others, or becomes frustrated when you become engrossed in a conversation that's not with her.
- If this is the case, acknowledge that you hear her frustration

  - *"You want me to talk to you, and you, only. That's frustrating."*
  - *"You would like a turn to speak. Is that right?"*

- Take time to create a "round robin" of conversation, wherein everyone has a chance and a distinguished turn to speak.

  - Make this into a ritualized event and take time at the beginning of a meal to go around the table and have a chance to talk to each other, or for each person to have the opportunity to share their thoughts.

SING

- When singing songs or nursery rhymes, give your child choices to allow her to feel involved and independent, and to help her anticipate what's coming next:

    - She can choose what songs to sing
    - She can choose *how* you'll adapt the song you'll sing about next

- Use pauses before you complete a phrase to prolong the inevitable, and build the anticipation:

    - This creates excitement and playfulness
    - Builds patience and attention
    - Plays with variety within a familiar pattern

MOVE

- Provide opportunities for your child to practice independent skills, whenever possible.
- Within daily routines (e.g., eating, toileting, dressing), slow down and give the time for your child to try something new.
- Learning to snap, zip or button for oneself, using an open cup, using a butter knife to "try" to cut... these are all ways for your child to grow:

    - Focused attention
    - Effortful control
    - Motor control
    - Adaptive (independent) skills

34 Months Old: Patterns Everywhere

Patterns Everywhere (Cognitive Development)

As your child starts to make more sense of the world around her, patterns begin to emerge. She starts to classify and categorize the pieces of her world, recognizing patterns in behavior, in people, in routines, in music, and in objects around her. These skills also require the ability to understand specific vocabulary, to visually distinguish between a few items or pictures, and to take in various aspects of objects in the environment (qualities like soft, big, short, etc).

Typically, young children start to develop emerging matching skills in toddlerhood, and match "like" objects. There are many concepts at play within this skill: understanding the concept of "same" vs. "different," an ability to visually distinguish between a number of items or pictures, the ability to sort and categorize by color, size, shape, texture, etc... Young children often begin to understand the meaning of these words and concepts before they are able to express them, so your child may surprise you when she suddenly makes a connection by pointing to or holding up an object you asked for in passing (even if you didn't realize she understood what you were talking about)!

The ability to match involves an ability to perceive and take in aspects of objects in the environment. The ability to begin to match "like" items also indicates that the young child is starting to discern and understand the world by classifying items in certain ways. Matching and classification are both related to the activity of sorting, in that young children are constantly organizing life experiences, new words, objects, and people, and determining how all these things relate to each other, and to themselves. Classification is essentially the grouping and sorting of various characteristics.

When young children start to explore, they begin to make classifications about their world, determining how certain things are alike and how they are different – through tactile experiences, visual, auditory, movement, and oral experiences.

WHAT YOU CAN DO:

Create opportunities for matching, categorizing, and patterning using images or objects in your environment.

PLAY

- Go inside and outside:
    - Play in and on various textures (e.g., dirt, sand, carpet, wood)
    - Play with variously textured objects (e.g., soft, hard, wet, dry)
    - Play with various colors, textures, sounds, and people

TALK

- Give your child *more* information about the items you're sorting, matching, or categorizing by describing them
    - e.g., *"All of these are food! Food is what we eat – yum!"*

SING

- Use a few "double" images
    - Printed twice from a web search
    - Finding two of the same object in a coupon mailer
    - Using two of the same magazine *(a great use of travel magazines found on an airplane)*

- Adapt a familiar tune (taking advantage of the natural patterning that is a familiar melody, and applying different words)
- Sing about "*Where the other ____*" is (I like to use the tune, "*Did You Ever See A Lassie?*"), creating a matching game.

Great Resource: Learn With Less DIY Blog post, "Travel Math & Music Activities For Toddlers"

MOVE

- Go on a scavenger hunt of your home, and find all the "like" objects in your home.

    ◦ Decide on a category in advance
    ◦ Give your child a choice between two acceptable options

        ▪ "Round" things
        ▪ Objects made of metal
        ▪ Things that fit inside an egg carton
        ▪ Fuzzy things
        ▪ Animals
        ▪ Things with wheels

34 Months Old: Building Narratives

Building Narratives (Communication Development)

When we talk about communication development, we include several areas, including the actual motor production of speech (the ability to articulate various sounds and sequence them together to create meaningful words and sentences), what a child understands or receives (receptive language), and finally a child's output, or what a child expresses (expressive language).

As your child approaches his third birthday, you may be wondering if he is "on track" for milestones related to communication. Each of the above areas (speech, receptive language, and expressive language) is related to your child's ability to interact with and understand the world around him, and express himself (not only to get his basic needs and desires met, but also to express his thoughts, ideas, and opinions). By three years, a child is typically able to sequence the sounds in words to be understood verbally at least 75% of the time to an unfamiliar listener,[26] able to put three words together to express himself,[27] and follow 2-3 step directions independently (e.g., go to the door, get your shoes, and bring them back to me).

As your child learns to participate in various aspects of a conversation (at this age, topics are often led by your child!), he will start to tell stories and build narrative abilities. He will likely focus on routines in which he regularly engages, or experiences that were notably out of a routine. As your child learns to tell a story, it's you who structures the environment for that narrative. You are the one asking questions, creating a space for your child to respond, and asking another question or offering more information to which your child responds. This also creates a feedback loop, and teaches your child about topic maintenance.

WHAT YOU CAN DO:

Talk about what you're doing, what's happening around you, about what you expect to do next, and about what happened recently (in the past). Sequence a story, process, or routine in all of its steps.

26. Pena-Brooks, Adriana, & Hedge, M.N. (2007). Assessment and treatment of articulation and phonological disorders in children (2nd edition). Austin, TX: PRO-ED.
27. Brown, R. (1973). A first language: The early stages. London: George Allen & Unwin.

PLAY

- Look at pictures or photographs in your environment (e.g., on the wall, in a book, in a magazine)
- Make inferences about:

    ◦ What might be happening
    ◦ Where the people are
    ◦ What the air might feel like
    ◦ What time of day it is

- Share your opinion, and ask your child for his.

Great Resource: **Learn With Less podcast episode, "How to Support Early Communication," featuring a discussion with San Francisco Moms Blog founder, Kelly Arditi**

TALK

- Wonder aloud about what might come next in a familiar routine or process, allowing your child to take the lead and communicate to you what he knows will happen.
- Talk about an event that happened in the recent past that was "unexpected" or out of the ordinary

    ◦ Ask questions about what happened "next" or "after that"

SING

- Sing about the process of what you're doing.

  - Use a familiar tune (a favorite of mine is "*Here We Go Round The Mulberry Bush*") to adapt the words of what you're doing first, next, and last.
  - For instance, if you're washing your hands, you might sing, "*First we're going to turn on the water, turn on the water, turn on the water...*").

MOVE

- Talk through the process of what you need to do to get out out of the house.

  - Look out the window to anticipate what clothes might be necessary
  - Ask your child where he might find a necessary tool you'll need to bring with you (e.g., the keys to the car, his flashlight, a walking stick)

35 Months Old: Movement Exploration

Movement Exploration (Motor Development)

It is the environment we create for our child that shapes their experience of learning and of life.[28] Research suggests that children of this

28. Dowshen, S., & Walter, R. (2001). The power of play. Available online: http://www.kidshealth.org

age should not be sedentary for more than one hour at a time, except while sleeping.[29] As your child learns more about her body and the way it moves, she also learns about the concepts involved in move-ment, such as directional concepts and spatial awareness (e.g., climb-ing up, through, between, etc), depth perception (e.g., knowing how far to throw a crumpled piece of paper to make it into the bowl), and hand-eye coordination (e.g., throwing a ball back to you).

When your child moves her body in different ways and for a good por-tion of the day, she builds core strength and stability. Her core muscles (those of the abdomen, back, and pelvis) support both her gross motor development and fine motor tasks, including her eventual ability to sit at a desk, have a strong base of support for tasks like handwriting, and even her ability to maintain attention and focus.[30]

WHAT YOU CAN DO:

Provide ample time for your child to be upright, and moving!

PLAY

- Dig holes in dirt or sand (with hands, sticks, shovels, stor-age containers, or spoons).
- Take turns blowing and chasing bubbles, or throwing and kicking a ball back and forth.

29. National Association for Sport and Physical Education. (2002). Active start: A statement of physical activity guidelines for children birth to five years. New York: AAHPERD Publications.
30. Diamond, A. & Lee, K. (2011). Interventions Shown to Aid Executive Function Development in Children 4 to 12 Years Old. Science 19 August 959-964

TALK

- Ask your child where she wants to race "to,"
    - Give her the opportunity to communicate to you the structure or physical representation of where the finish line will be

SING

- Make regular time for dance parties!
    - Get silly together, and move to the rhythm of the music
- Make instruments out of the laundry basket and other simple percussive materials.

MOVE

- Get your child's help with household tasks like:
    - Sorting laundry
    - Emptying garbage
    - Cleaning up toys
    - Pushing a shopping cart
    - Climbing into the car seat independently

35 Months Old: Toy Rotation

Toy Rotation (Social/Emotional Development)

We all hope for our children to become independent – in play, in daily tasks, in knowing how to behave in situations. Setting up the environment for our children to access open-ended materials with which they can explore and investigate the world creates an atmosphere in which they are more likely to become both independent thinkers and independent actors.

We can think about creating access to the environment through both the physical space itself (e.g., your child has access to an area in which she can explore independently) as well as the content (e.g., what types of objects and how many objects are available – quality as well as quantity). This is where the notion of "repetition with variation" comes into play. When a large number of toys are always available, and or the function of each toy is similar, your child's attention and interest in her playthings may appear to diminish.

When play materials then reappear after being absent, your child is more likely to perceive them as novel "stimuli" – and therefore, she is more likely to be interested in them, and likely to explore them more fully. Your child also may be more likely to experiment or play with two previously unrelated objects (e.g., building wooden block homes for her plastic animals, or creating car tire tracks with paint on her paper).

WHAT YOU CAN DO:

Think of your play materials in terms of their function (e.g., building toys, art or "messy" play materials, literacy materials, physical activity toys, musical toys, dramatic play toys, pretend play toys, etc), and limit the number of each. Try to ensure that no more than one toy within each category is available at any given time.

These are not "hard and fast" categories; rather, they are meant to help you start thinking about how your child might play with different objects.

PLAY

- If you don't have the space to actually "remove" toys from the environment, try minimizing the visual appeal of certain toys (by covering them or placing them behind other objects) or by highlighting other objects in the environment, making them more interesting.
- Create an interesting "tableau" for your child to wake up to in the morning, wherein specific toys are set up in ways that might tempt her to explore them further (e.g., a paper roll is affixed to the wall with a piece of tape, next to a bowl of various objects that might fit through it).

Great Resource: **Learn With Less podcast episode, "Bringing Montessori Home,"** featuring an interview with Montessori educator and consultant, Jeanne-Marie Paynel

TALK

- Observe what your child does and how she plays with objects.
- Make comments about what she's doing, ask for a turn, or model something different and talk about what was different about it.

SING

- Rotate musical toys in and out of your child's environment, remembering that musical instruments can be

made out of – or combined with – nearly anything!
- Creating musical experiences or playing with musical toys doesn't always have to be about playing music together.

  - Count the instruments
  - Find all the instruments or objects (from various categories) that are a similar shape or that make a similar sound

Great Resource: Learn With Less podcast episode, "How to Support Your Infant or Toddler's Development Without Going Crazy," featuring speech-language pathologist and founder of "The Speech Mom," Andrea Boerigter

MOVE

- When there is a place for everything, everything has its place.

  - By categorizing play materials, your child also learns to categorize.

- Encourage your child to help you put things away when it's time to transition to the next activity

  - Create a routine around cleaning up
  - Ask her where and how things go away
  - Create the opportunity for her to be independent and to take charge

36 Months Old: Executive Functioning

Executive Functioning (Cognitive Development)

The skills we use to get through difficult situations, manage our emotions, plan ahead, focus on tasks at hand, show patience, and make valid and reasonable judgment calls (yes, exactly, all the skills with which toddlers struggle) are known as "executive functioning" skills. We can think of them as the skills a business executive would need to be successful. The fact is, toddlers are not able to hold down a job, behave as executives (though your child might argue about who's "in charge"), and do things like plan ahead... precisely because the area of the brain which is responsible for this set of skills (the frontal lobe) is not yet fully developed. The truth of the matter is that it will not be fully developed until your child is approximately 22 years old.[31]

Though we cannot expect our toddlers to have mastered these skills, there are things we can do to help our children develop them. Research suggests that executive functioning skills can be developed through the establishment of routines, by modeling positive social behavior, and by maintaining supportive and consistently reliable relationships.

WHAT YOU CAN DO:

Create opportunities for problem-solving, flexible thinking, and following through with tasks by giving your child an opportunity to participate in the activities of the day at her level.

PLAY

31. Johnson, S. B., Blum, R. W., & Giedd, J. N. (2009). Adolescent maturity and the brain: the promise and pitfalls of neuroscience research in adolescent health policy. The Journal of adolescent health : official publication of the Society for Adolescent Medicine, 45(3), 216-21.

- Provide visual supports (picture books, photos in the environment) representing the routines, people, animals, household and other familiar objects.

    ◦ Provide opportunities to talk about those pictures

- Make connections between what she knows about the world and what she does in the world
- Connect with stories:

    ◦ Past experiences
    ◦ Familiar experiences
    ◦ Actions
    ◦ Events (both novel and routine)
    ◦ People
    ◦ Objects
    ◦ Places

Great Resource: **Learn With Less podcast episode, "Learning, Executive Functioning, and Play,"** featuring an interview with early childhood educator Renee Peña Lopez

TALK

- In a social situation, try to frame the sharing of objects as turn taking rather than "giving" an object to another person.
- Guide your child through her emotions by talking through the experience

    ◦ *"It's really hard – you want to play with that car... but right now your friend is playing with it. Let's try this one and then ask for a turn again in a few minutes"*

- Provide alternative ideas for play or social problem-solving guidance.

SING

- When anticipating a transition between activities, use a familiar melody to "mark" that transition.
  - A good-bye song or clean up song can be very helpful to help your child prepare herself for a shift in activity.
  - This might be a simple counting song
    - You sing or tap a rhythm to the numbers as you count to 10
    - A timer used to count down at the "one more minute" mark that ends in the playing of a familiar or preferred song.

MOVE

- Give your child a "mission" – framing the provision of one-step or two-step directions as a special task with which she gets to help, or which only she gets to complete.
- Creating opportunities for your child to feel useful and independent (e.g., *"Ok, ready? I need you to... grab that shirt and throw in the laundry hamper. Then come back to me. Ready? Go!"*)

> ◦ It also allows her to:
>
>> ▪ Use her working memory
>> ▪ Focus her attention
>> ▪ Follow through with a plan of action from start to finish

36 Months Old: Communication Awareness

Communication Awareness (Communicative Development)

Each time you communicate with your child, you either teach about something new and unfamiliar, or reinforce something familiar (e.g., a pattern of behavior, a concept and how things are connected, a vocabulary word). As time goes on, your child learns to use more verbal language and will rely on gestures less; however, we all use multiple modes to communicate (verbal as well as nonverbal communication), and to clarify information.

By the age of three years old, your child (whether he's been exposed to one language or multiple languages) is able to alter his style of communication depending on his communication partner. This switching of styles is known as "code switching," and can be seen when switching from one language to another (the metalinguistic awareness of with whom to use which language), when speaking to adults vs. other children (e.g., including, for instance, "polite" words), and even between same-aged vs. younger peers. Typically, a three-year old will modify his communication style when communicating with an infant, with someone who speaks a different language, or with someone who exhibits communication delays. This is exemplified by the child using additional gestures, as well as features of infant-directed speech (such as a slowed rate, more exaggerated pitch contours, more repetition and shorter utterances).

WHAT YOU CAN DO:

These modifications are a reflection of your child's ability to take another person's perspective, and inferring what another person needs to know for them to understand.

PLAY

- When engaging in pretend play scenarios, encourage inference-making by asking your child what might need to happen next, making "if; then" statements.
- Perform caregiving routines with a stuffed animal or baby doll (e.g., bathing, feeding, diaper change).
- If all you have is a paper and pen or a magazine handy, draw simple pictures or act out scenarios with magazine photographs.

TALK

- Typically, a child of this age is able to express his wants and desires, and his emotions will be quite obvious.
- The more you can provide emotional vocabulary around what your child is feeling and what he needs, the more he will be able to eventually express himself emotionally.
- His ability to express the physical state of what's happening (*e.g., "my bear!"*) will, in time, become about the mental or emotional state (*e.g., "I'm mad! I want that bear"*).

SING

- When singing songs or engaging in finger plays, act out the movements that might represent a word (e.g., actions, feelings)

  - Continue to link the vocabulary with a gestural experience, providing multiple modes of expression.

MOVE

- Take on the movements of different animals

  - Walk or move like a bear, make the sounds
  - Encourage your child to assume the physical characteristics of someone else

Where to go from here

The ideas in this book are simple for a reason: you already have everything it takes to support your child. Sometimes it simply takes a bit of hand-holding and a friendly fist bump from another parent who's been through the trenches (and who knows that there's no right or wrong way to be a parent). Regardless of how many – or how few – of the modules you've gone through, I sincerely hope the information within this book has provided you with a good place to start when it comes to interacting with and learning about your toddler.

If you enjoyed Understanding Your Toddler, I hope you'll take a moment to review it on Amazon. This will help other parents, caregivers, and professionals working with families find resources that help them. In fact, I hope you'll share this book with your friends or family who have (or will have!) toddlers. Along with the bestselling book Understanding Your Baby, these books provide the perfect gift for any new (or newish) parent – after all, what better gift could you give a new or expecting parent than the gift of knowledge?

The learning doesn't stop here. We weren't meant to parent in isolation! Readers of Understanding Your Baby and Understanding Your Toddler, and followers of Learn With Less®, report greater satisfaction and more embracive results within the context of our parent education and parent support platform, the Learn With Less® Curriculum Online Program. The program is a virtual content platform and community for families and professionals working with infants and toddlers of all developmental levels.

Inside, you'll find resources around:

- **Understanding infant and toddler development**, with deeper access to our full developmental curriculum, and with additional commentary and video examples
- **Planning activities that support development**, using our four-pillar framework (Play, Talk, Sing, Move) within each module in

both *Understanding Your Baby* and *Understanding Your Toddler*
- **Making more with less**, addressing the universal lack of time and energy many parents experience, showing you how to maximize routines and open-ended materials
- **Balancing needs, priorities, and relationships** (self-care, developmental needs, home priorities, etc.)
- **Setting limits**, and ideas for discipline, with regard to self-regulation for both the parent and child
- **Setting up the environment for learning**, encouraging independent play and emotional intelligence
- **"Am I Doing It Right?,"** empowering parents through live virtual support groups that include "hot seats" and address *your* questions and challenges

If this sounds like a place you'd like to experience, come find us at learnwithless.com/online.

Want in-person connection? Check to see if one of our licensed Learn With Less® facilitators is hosting classes or workshops in your area! You can find a list of current providers here: https://learnwithless.com/classes

We are a generous, caring community of families and professionals that values good citizenship, diversity in perspectives, and respectful interactions.

Wishing you more great moments with what counts,

Ayelet Marinovich

https://learnwithless.com

Made in the USA
Las Vegas, NV
26 July 2023

75281729R00095